PALM

DE MALLORCA

TRAVEL GUIDE

Unveiling the Charms of Palma de Mallorca: Your Ultimate Travel Companion

LEONARDO JOBS

Copyright © 2023, Leonardo Jobs

TABLE OF CONTENTS

INTRODUCTION

Journey of Dream and Determination: Natalie's Odyssey to Palma de Mallorca

Natalie found herself longing for a getaway from the dull routine and constant commotion of everyday life. She longed for an escape from the same routine that had kept her confined for far too long. She felt drawn to the attraction of adventure by its seductive whispers of fresh encounters, foreign vistas, and the addictive rush of discovery. She set out to organise her ideal vacation to Palma de Mallorca with unyielding tenacity.

Natalie's trip into the centre of Palma de Mallorca was an adventure in and of itself, full with expectation and excitement. It was a journey that started with the straightforward act of opening her laptop and entering those miraculous words. She immersed herself in a virtual world of travel blogs, travel manuals, as well as my social media post that centred on how to plan a trip to Palma de Mallorca, and enticing tales of intrepid companions who had travelled to the Mediterranean jewel that was Palma with a fervour only matched by the intensity of her yearning.

Her dependable travel notepad was loaded to the brim with notes. As she painstakingly created her idealised version of the ideal Palma vacation, lists were made, itineraries were created, and inspiration poured. In order to discover the secrets hidden behind this alluring location's sun-kissed surface, Natalie set out to understand its essence.

Her journey started with culture and history. She dove into Palma's history, entwining herself in the tales of the ancient cultures that had left a lasting impression on the island. More than just tourist attractions, the centuries-old cathedrals, the maze-like streets of the Old Town, and the swaying palm trees along the coastal promenade become parts of a living history.

Practicalities followed as Natalie focused on the organisation of her adventure. She carefully considered when to go and determined the best time of year to travel. She carefully examined her spending, wanting to make every dollar matter. The packing list started to take shape as well as the visa applications and travel insurance.

She had to figure out transportation by comparing and evaluating several airline alternatives until she discovered the best one that would whisk her off to Palma. She explored the complexities of the city's public transport, the ease of hiring a bicycle, and the appeal of taking leisurely strolls through the quaint streets.

Another aspect of her thorough planning involved accommodations. Natalie browsed a wide range of web postings, perused several reviews, and imagined herself in each potential hotel. She yearned for her decision to be more than simply a bed; she wanted it to be a haven of comfort and a starting point for her excursions on Palma.

There were difficulties on the way to Palma de Mallorca. Moments of doubt, the weight of the judgements that needed to be taken, and the sporadic pre-trip butterflies all existed. But Natalie's resolve stayed unwavering throughout it all. She realised that this trip was an opportunity for self-discovery and personal development, not just a simple change of scenery.

Join Natalie on an enthralling adventure as she steps off the plane in Palma de Mallorca, eager to embrace the unknown, savour regional cuisine, and unearth hidden treasures in the Mediterranean's embrace. We will travel Palma's twisting streets side by side, absorbing its rich history, culture, and lively energy as we go. We will be walking in her footsteps. This is the account of Natalie's meticulously prepared and anxiously anticipated getaway to Palma de Mallorca, a trip that holds the promise of adventure, personal development, and the making of priceless memories that will last a lifetime.

CHAPTER 1

Getting to Know Palma de Mallorca

Palma de Mallorca, the capital of the Balearic Islands, invites visitors with its distinctive fusion of history, culture, and natural beauty as it is tucked away like a priceless pearl in the centre of the Mediterranean. It's important to familiarise yourself with Palma's spirit before travelling to this magical city, where every cobblestone street has a tale to tell and every moment holds the possibility of discovery.

A Peek into Culture and History:

The history of Palma spans millennia and has seen the emergence and fall of numerous civilizations. This alluring island bears the imprint of Phoenicians, Romans, Moors, and Christians.

The city's origins may be found in the Roman era, when it was known as "Palmaria Palma." It eventually came under Moorish dominion and took the name "Medina Mayurqa."

A turning point was reached when King James I of Aragon regained the city during the Christian Reconquista in the 13th century.

The Palma Cathedral, also known as **"La Seu"** locally, is the architectural jewel of the city and a reminder of its Gothic heritage.

Its soaring spires and intricate rose window reflect centuries of craftsmanship and devotion.

Explore the bustling art scene and the thriving music and dance traditions to fully experience Palma's rich culture. Palma provides a sensual tapestry of artistic expression, whether you're exploring modern art galleries or savouring the ferocious rhythms of traditional Flamenco.

- **Experiencing Local Cuisine:**

Without sampling Palma's wonderful cuisine, your tour would be incomplete. Palma offers a culinary experience that combines innovation and heritage. Enjoy some fresh seafood, try the traditional "sobrassada" sausage, then wash it all down with some crisp Mallorcan wine. Here, eating is more than simply a means of subsistence; it's a celebration of tastes and customs.

- **Amazing architectural feats**

The Palma Cathedral, colloquially known as "La Seu," is one of Palma's most recognisable structures and a reminder of its Gothic past. The cathedral was built over several decades, starting in the 13th century, and is now considered a masterpiece of architecture. Awe-inspiring features include its beautiful rose window, soaring buttresses, and elaborate interior details.

You will come upon a maze of little lanes, secret courtyards, and lovely squares as you meander around Palma's Old Town's charming streets. The city's cultural development may be seen in the ancient architecture, which combines Moorish, Gothic, and Baroque elements.

- **Culture and the Arts:**

In Palma's many galleries and museums, the artistic spirit is alive and well. A substantial collection of modern Balearic and Spanish art is on display in the Es Baluard modern Art Museum. Outside of its borders, sculptures and graffiti art adorn public areas, transforming them into a welcoming urban gallery.

The city's cultural calendar is jam-packed with occasions and festivals that honour its history.

Both the lively Sant Joan festival and the Fiestas de San Sebastián, which bring the city to life with music, dance, and traditional processions, are not to be missed.

- **An Everlasting Legacy:**

The history and culture of Palma de Mallorca are not just present in its museums and monuments; they also permeate citizens' day-to-day activities. It's a place where historical architecture and modern art coexist together, where the spirit of culture is alive and well in the city's bustling streets. You will embark on a voyage through time as you delve into Palma's history and culture and learn about the timeless qualities that make this Mediterranean treasure so alluring.

Geography and Climate

- **Geographical Wonders:**

The topography of Palma is a masterpiece of mother nature. To the northwest of the city, the Serra de Tramuntana mountain range embraces it, providing a spectacular backdrop of jagged peaks that seem to reach the sky. These mountains offer a haven for hikers and environment lovers in addition to adding to the city's stunning scenery.

A coastline dotted with some of the most immaculate beaches in the Mediterranean stretches south and east of Palma. The island's coasts are softly lapped by the turquoise waves of the Mediterranean, offering countless options for sunbathing, water sports, and relaxation. Playa de Palma and Cala Mayor are two of the most well-known beaches, each giving a certain attraction and charm.

- **Mediterranean Climate**

With moderate, rainy winters and scorching, dry summers, Palma de Mallorca experiences a Mediterranean climate. The city enjoys over 300 days of sunshine each year, making it a year-round destination for visitors seeking good weather.

I. **Spring:**

Palma celebrates the renewal of nature in the springtime. The city's parks and gardens blossom in vibrant colour, and the temperature starts to rise, with typical highs between 17°C and 21°C (63°F and 70°F)

II.   Summer:

With July and August being the warmest months, summer is when Palma is at its most alluring. 29°C to 31°C (84°F to 88°F) is the typical high temperature range for these months. The city's colourful environment is brought to life by outdoor events and festivals, which draw beachgoers and fans of water sports.

III.   Autumn:

With highs in Palma ranging from 24°C to 27°C (75°F to 81°F) as summer gives way to autumn, the island of Mallorca experiences cooler temperatures. The city's cultural attractions can be enjoyed during this time of year, and you can avoid the summertime crowds by participating in outdoor activities.

IV.   Winter:

High temperatures in Palma's winters typically range from 15°C to 17°C (59°F to 63°F). Despite not being a typical winter paradise, the city's cultural attractions, such as its museums and historical buildings, continue to draw tourists even in the colder months.

- **A Year-Round Paradise:**

For those looking for both natural beauty and pleasant weather, Palma de Mallorca's topography and climate combine to create a paradise. Palma's geographical wonders and Mediterranean climate guarantee that your trip will be nothing short of enjoyable whether you arrive in the warm and calm winter months or the summer's sun-drenched days.

Local Cuisine

- **Savoring Seafood:**

It should come as no surprise that Palma's cuisine emphasises seafood given its coastal location. The tables of neighbourhood eateries are adorned with fresh catches of fish and shellfish, frequently obtained from the waters close to the island. Rich lobster stew called "Caldereta de Langosta," a must-try dish that embodies the island's passion for fish. It is a delicious testimony to the abundance of the Mediterranean when simmered in a flavorful tomato-based broth.

- **Delicious Meat Dishes:**

Beyond seafood, the cuisine of Palma features a wide variety of meat dishes to suit any taste. A well-known regional delicacy called **"sobrassada"** is a Mallorcan sausage made with ground pig, paprika, and spices. It can be enjoyed in meals like **"Tumbet,"** a delicious vegetable and potato casserole, or spread on crusty toast.

- **Embracing Local Produce:**

Mallorca's fertile lands yield an abundance of fresh produce that inspires the island's cuisine. The humble **"pa amb oli"** is a beloved Mallorcan snack consisting of crusty bread drizzled with olive oil and topped with tomatoes, garlic, and a pinch of sea salt. It exemplifies the island's emphasis on simplicity and the use of top-quality ingredients.

- **Consuming Desserts:**

Without a sweet treat to please the palette, no lunch in Mallorca is considered complete. The beloved delicacy **"ensaimada,"** a coiled pastry sprinkled with powdered sugar, has become a recognised representation of Palma's culinary tradition. For a lovely afternoon break, serve it with a "café con leche."

- **Spirits and wine:**

The wine industry of Palma de Mallorca is also growing and produces a wide range of wines, including reds, whites, and rosés. Try some local wines while you're in Palma, such those from the Pla i Llevant and Binissalem-Mallorca regions. Don't pass up the chance to sample **"hierbas,"** a conventional herbal liqueur frequently consumed as a **digestif.**

- **Dining Experiences:**

The dining options in Palma range from inexpensive tapas bars to Michelin-starred establishments. If you stroll through the city's old streets, you'll come across quaint, family-run businesses that serve food made from recipes that have been developed over many generations.

- **Market Delights:**

Explore the vibrant markets of Palma, such as the Mercat de Santa Catalina and Mercat de l'Olivar, for a true culinary immersion. Fresh fruit, meats, cheeses, and seafood are displayed at these bright marketplaces in a variety of vibrant ways. Interact with local sellers, try their wares, and perhaps even buy some ingredients to prepare your own cuisine with a Mallorcan flair at home.

Language and Communication

Official Languages:

- **Spanish (Castilian):** The official and most common language on the entire island, including Palma de Mallorca, is Spanish (Castilian). Speaking Spanish well will make it easy for visitors to go around the city, interact with the populace, and ask for help when they need it.

- **Catalan:** The Balearic Islands also have the Mallorqui dialect of Catalan as an official language. Despite being widely used, it is mainly employed in more formal settings, such as court cases and official documents. Mallorque is a charming dialect that is frequently used by locals, so hearing it will enhance the authenticity of your trip.

- **English:** In Palma, especially in tourist-heavy regions, English is frequently spoken and understood. Many locals, especially those working in the service sector, are fluent in English, making it simple for tourists who speak that language to interact and get help.

- **Other Languages:** Due to Palma's appeal on a global scale, you'll meet individuals from all over the world. As a result, both locals and visitors may speak in various languages. Due to the city's popularity with European tourists, German and French are among the languages that are more frequently heard.

Getting Around Language Strictures:

In Palma de Mallorca, especially in tourist areas, language difficulties are typically not a major issue, but knowing a few simple Spanish words can greatly improve your trip and help you interact with people. Even if you mostly communicate in English, showing politeness and making an attempt to speak the local tongue is frequently appreciated.

Respect for diversity:

The language and culture of Mallorca are very important to the people there. Interactions with locals can be more meaningful and one can gain a deeper understanding of their culture by demonstrating an interest in their way of life and

SOME COMMON PALMA MALLORCAN WORDS:

Hola: Hello

Adéu: Goodbye

Gràcies: Thank you

De res: You're welcome

Perdó: Excuse me

Estàs bé?: Are you okay?

Molt bé, gràcies: Very well, thank you

Encantat/a de conèixer-te: Nice to meet you

Com estàs?: How are you?

No parlo català: I don't speak Catalan

Parla anglès?: Do you speak English?

Here are some other useful words and phrases:

L'hotel: The hotel

El restaurant: The restaurant

El bar: The bar

El metro: The metro

El tren: The train

El mapa: The map

El comerç: The shop

La platja: The beach

El centre de la ciutat: The city center

El bus: The bus

El taxi: The taxi

exhibiting respect for their traditions, including their language.

Optimising Your Visit:

Consider learning some basic Spanish before going to Palma de Mallorca. This effort can improve your trip, provide opportunities for real cultural exchanges, and deepen your comprehension of the city and its residents.

Currency and Practical Information

- **Currency Exchange:**

In Palma de Mallorca, there are many places to exchange money, mainly in the city centre and the airport. You may readily receive euros thanks to the accessibility of banks, exchange offices, and ATMs. Major credit and debit cards are also frequently accepted in hotels, eateries, retail establishments, and tourist sites.

ATMs:

In Palma de Mallorca, which is called **"cajeros automáticos"** in Spanish, ATMs are widely available.

They provide a simple way to withdraw euros. To save transaction costs, be sure to inquire with your bank or financial institution about any fees related to overseas ATM withdrawals.

Credit Cards:

In Palma de Mallorca, credit cards including Visa, MasterCard, and American Express are widely accepted. To avoid any problems using your card outside of the country, it is advisable to let your bank know about your trip intentions. The majority of businesses, including hotels, restaurants, and shops, favour card payments, making it a practical option for tourists.

Tipping:

Though not required, tipping is traditional in Palma de Mallorca. If service is not included in the price, it is traditional to give a tip in restaurants of between 5% and 10% of the total. Be sure to check the bill before adding an additional tip because in upmarket establishments, service charges could be automatically included.

Shopping Hours:

Although Palma de Mallorca's retail establishments may operate during a variety of hours, most are open from 10:00 AM to 8:00 PM, with a siesta break in the early afternoon. Planning your shopping carefully will help you avoid disappointment on Sundays and major holidays. Restaurants and other facilities catering to tourists, on the other hand, generally stay open all day.

Time zone:

CET, or UTC+1, is the time zone used in Palma de Mallorca. It adheres to Central European Summer Time **(CEST),** which is **UTC+2**, when in daylight saving time (usually from the last Sunday in March to the last Sunday in October).

Visa requirement:

The Schengen Area includes all of Spain, including Palma de Mallorca. You might need to get a Schengen visa ahead of time depending on your nationality. Check the laws and rules pertaining to visas in your country of residence well in advance of your trip.

Emergency Services:

To contact police, medical, or fire services in an emergency, dial 112, the emergency number for Europe.

Electricity:

Type C and Type F Europlug electrical outlets are used across Spain, including Palma de Mallorca. **50Hz** and **230V** are the standard frequency and voltage, respectively. Travellers from nations with various plug types may require a travel adaptor to charge their electronics.

CHAPTER 2

Planning Your Trip

A plan is the first step of every journey, no matter how short or long. Your journeys are steered by the map, and new horizons are discovered by following the compass. Whether you're travelling to a far-off place or exploring your own backyard, a guide is a necessity.

This guide is your travel companion, offering insights, advice, and inspiration to help you create unforgettable experiences, make lasting memories, and set out on the journey of a lifetime to the magnificent city of Palma de Mallorca. Consequently, let's start the process of organising your trip, where every decision is a chance for learning and every second is an opportunity to see the city's wonders.

When to Visit

- **Spring (March to May):**

The City comes to life in the spring with a burst of colour and life. Exploring outside is made possible by the warm climate, which ranges from **17°C to 21°C (63°F to 70°F).**

When hiking, riding, or simply taking a leisurely stroll through the old streets, the island's verdant surroundings are in full bloom and provide a beautiful backdrop.

For those looking for a quiet getaway with fewer people, this season is ideal.

- **Summer (June to August):**

Palma de Mallorca's summers are known for their sunny days and energetic celebrations. The temperature rises to its highest point, with daily highs typically ranging from 84°F to 88°F (29°C to 31°C). This is peak tourist season, when the city comes to life with outdoor events, festivals, and nightlife, and the beaches are bustling with activity. This is the perfect time to travel if you've been dreaming of a traditional Mediterranean beach vacation.

- **Autumn (September to November):**

The cooler autumn temperatures, which range from 24°C to 27°C (75°F to 81°F), deliver a soothing change from the oppressive summer heat. Without the summertime crowds, it's a wonderful time of year to explore Palma's cultural attractions, like as its museums and historical monuments.

The city's culinary sector is still thriving, and the coastline remains tempting for swimming and other water activities.

- **Winter (December to February):**

Despite not being a typical winter destination, Palma de Mallorca has a warm winter climate, with average highs of 15°C to 17°C (59°F to 63°F). Travellers looking for a more sedate and cheap experience should go during the winter. There are less tourists, so you may enjoy the city's lovely streets, delectable local fare, and cultural events. It's also a great time to go hiking in the scenic mountains of the island.

The ideal time to travel to Palma de Mallorca ultimately depends on your interests and the kind of experience you're looking for. Palma greets you with open arms and promises a Mediterranean paradise for every season, whether you're drawn to the exuberant energy of summer, the tranquility of spring, the cultural riches of autumn, or the peace of winter.

Budgeting and Costs

A. **Accommodation:** Finding Budget-Friendly Stays:

The cost of lodging frequently makes up a sizable amount of your travel spending. But Palma de Mallorca offers a variety of hotel choices to fit different price ranges.

I. **Hostels:** Numerous hostels in Palma offer affordable housing in a clean, comfortable dorm-style setting. The common kitchens in these hostels make it simple to prepare your meals and cut back on dining prices.

II. **Guesthouses and Bed & Breakfasts:** These lodging options are great for travellers on a tight budget. You can locate quaint, locally owned buildings that provide an intimate and genuine experience without the high cost of luxury hotels.

III. **Short-Term Rentals:** Numerous reasonably priced flats and studios are available in Palma on websites like Airbnb and Vrbo. They provide you the opportunity to experience a more cosy setting while also giving you the option to prepare your own meals to cut down on the cost of eating out.

IV.   **Camping:** For those with a sense of adventure, think about camping in designated places. Camping may be an affordable way to get close to nature, and Mallorca has some lovely campgrounds.

B. **Using Transport to Get Around Cheaply:**

Despite the fact that they can rise, there are strategies to keep transport expenses under check:

I.   **Public transport:** Palma has a reliable system of buses and trams that can get you wherever in the city and to adjacent places. If you intend to use public transport regularly and want to save money, think about buying a travel card or pass.

II.   **Bicycles:** Renting a bicycle is an inexpensive and environmentally beneficial method to tour Palma and its surrounds. The city has designated cycling lanes, and there are several bike rental shops with affordable pricing.

III.   **Walking:** Palma's historic district is small and accessible by foot. Not only is it cheap to stroll through its little streets and alleyways, but it's also a great method to find hidden treasures.

C. Eating on a Budget and Enjoying Local Flavours:

Any budget can enjoy the culinary adventure Palma de Mallorca has to offer:

- **Local Markets:** Visit neighbourhood markets where you can buy fresh vegetables, cheese, and other supplies, such Mercat de l'Olivar and Mercat de Santa Catalina. Create your own picnic or eat at one of the market's food stands for a reasonable price.

- **Menu del Dia:** During lunchtime, several restaurants in Palma serve a "menu del dia" or "menu of the day." These fixed-price menus offer exceptional value because they often include an appetiser, entrée, dessert, and occasionally a drink.

- **Tapas and Pinchos:** Select bars that serve tapas and pinchos so you can sample a range of tiny foods for reasonable costs. It might be affordable and fun to eat out by splitting a few plates with friends.

- **Street Food:** Be on the lookout for street food sellers serving classic treats like "empanadas" and "bocadillos" (sandwiches).

With these reasonably priced snacks, you may sample regional flavours on the road.

D. Activities: Budget-Friendly Palma Exploration:

The cultural and ecological attractions of Palma don't have to break the bank to be explored:

- **Free Attractions:** Palma has a number of free sights to see, including the magnificent Palma Cathedral and the lovely **Parc de la Mar**, which offers wonderful views of both the sea and the cathedral.

- **Museums & Discounts:** You should schedule your trips according to the days and times that some museums provide free entry. Additionally, take a look at passes or discount cards that offer discounted entrance to a number of sites.

- **Outdoor Adventures:** Feel free to explore the island's natural beauties. For an affordable dose of adventure, hike the **Serra de Tramuntana**, unwind on the beaches or take a lovely drive along the coast.

E. Making the Most of Your Money with Budgeting Advice:

- **Plan ahead:** Do your homework and make an agenda in advance, taking advantage of deals and free activities.

- **Create a Daily Budget:** To keep you on target and prevent overspending, set a daily spending cap.

- **Use the Local Currency:** To avoid additional conversion fees, choose to pay in the local currency while making transactions.

- **Cook Some of Your Meals:** If your lodging permits, prepare some of your meals to reduce your dining expenses.

- Avoid tourist traps by seeking out neighbourhood eateries, markets, and shops outside of touristy districts where costs may be exaggerated.

Visa and Entry Requirements

I. Schengen Accord

The Schengen Agreement, which permits passport-free travel throughout much of Europe, applies to Palma de Mallorca because it is a part of Spain. For stays of up to 90 days within a 180-day period, no visa is necessary if you are a citizen of a Schengen Area member country and you can enter Palma de Mallorca with just your national ID or passport. Citizens of numerous European nations are affected by this.

II.   Visa-Exempt Nations:

When visiting Palma de Mallorca for brief stays, citizens of some non-Schengen nations are also not required to have a visa. The list of nations that don't require visas is subject to change, so for the most recent information, be sure you contact the Spanish consulate or embassy in your nation or visit the official Spanish government website.

III.   Visa requirements

If you are not a resident of a nation that is a member of the Schengen Area or one that is exempt from visa requirements, you might need a Schengen visa to visit Palma de Mallorca. Schengen visas are often provided for brief stays related to tourism, business, family visits, or other types of short stays.

In order to be eligible for a Schengen visa, you must;

I.   Fill out the visa application: Fill out the Schengen visa application form, which is accessible on the website of the Spanish consulate or embassy in your country.

II. Assemble the Necessary Documents: Usually, you must submit the following paperwork:

❖ A passport that is still valid and has at least two blank pages.

❖ Passport-sized pictures that adhere to certain specifications.

❖ Flight reservations are included in the travel schedule.

❖ Hotel bookings or a letter of invitation from a host are acceptable forms of documentation for proof of lodging in Palma de Mallorca.

❖ A sponsorship letter or bank statements are acceptable forms of proof of sufficient funds to finance your stay.

❖ Health and repatriation insurance for travellers with a minimum coverage of €30,000.

❖ Evidence of your nation of origin, such as a letter from your employment or ownership documents.

III. Make an appointment: To make an appointment for a visa interview, get in touch with the Spanish consulate or embassy in your nation. Be prepared to pay a visa application fee, which varies based on your country of citizenship.

IV. Attend the Visa Interview: Show up for your visa interview at the embassy or consulate. You can be questioned about the goal of your vacation and your intentions for Palma de Mallorca during the interview.

V. Wait for Processing: Because processing times for visas might vary, it's best to apply well in advance of the day you want to go. Your visa application may in some circumstances take several weeks to process.

VI. Once your visa has been issued, you must pick it up in person from the consulate or embassy. Verify the exact conditions for obtaining a visa in your country of residence.

Travel Insurance

The Importance of Travel Insurance:

- **Medical Coverage:** Illnesses and accidents can strike anybody, anywhere, at any time. Travel insurance guarantees that you will receive the required medical care without having to pay astronomical prices. It includes hospitalisation, doctor visits, prescriptions, and, if necessary, emergency medical evacuation.

- **Cancellation of Trip:** Since life is unpredictable, things can change. If you need to cancel your trip due to unforeseeable events like illness, family emergencies, or unforeseen business commitments, travel insurance can help you get reimbursed for non-refundable trip costs.

- **Trip Interruption:** Travel insurance can pay for the costs of rescheduling flights, lodging, and other pre-paid charges if your trip is cut short due to an unforeseen circumstance, such as a family emergency or severe weather interruptions.

- **Lost or Delayed Luggage:** On occasion, airlines lose luggage or encounter delivery delays for luggage. Until your luggage is found, your travel insurance may be able to reimburse you for clothing and other necessities.

- **Travel delays:** While they can be annoying, delays in transportation may be covered by travel insurance. These extra costs may include meals, lodging, and transportation.

- **Emergency aid:** Emergency aid services are frequently covered by travel insurance. This implies that you can get assistance with a variety of problems, such as missing passports or urgent legal counsel, whenever you need it and wherever you are.

Deciding on the Best Policy:

The following should be taken into account while choosing travel insurance for your trip to Palma de Mallorca:

- **Coverage limitations:** Specifically for travel and medical expenses, make sure the coverage limitations are adequate to satisfy your demands.

- **Pre-Existing issues:** Inform the insurance carrier of any pre-existing medical issues and learn how, if at all, they are covered.

- **Adventure Activities:** Make sure your insurance coverage covers them if you intend to partake in any adventure sports or activities. Additional protection could be needed for some activities.

- **Cancellation Reasons:** Review the policy's list of acceptable cancellation grounds to determine the situations that are protected.

- **Exclusions:** Carefully read the policy's exclusions to see what is not covered. Extreme sports, terrorism, and particular medical issues are a few common exclusions.

- **Claim Procedures:** Know the claim procedures, including the documentation required and the deadlines for filing claims.

- **Peace of Mind for Your Adventure in Palma:**

Travel insurance makes sure that you can enjoy exploring this Mediterranean treasure knowing that you are financially secure in the event of the unexpected.

Investigate your insurance options before leaving, pick the one that best meets your requirements, and travel with confidence that your vacation will be one to remember for all the right reasons.

CHAPTER 3

Getting Around Palma de Mallorca

Knowing how to get around the city is a necessary part of your adventure as you set out to see this gem of the Mediterranean. We'll walk you through the different ways to get around Palma de Mallorca, from taking the public transit to biking through gorgeous roads, guaranteeing that you can visit every part of this paradise.

Public Transportation

- **Public Buses:**

The city's public bus system, run by EMT (Empresa Municipal de Transportes), is a practical and economical means to get around Palma. Palma and its surroundings, including well-known tourist attractions, are serviced by the bus network. There are several different fare options available for buying tickets, which can be done on board or at kiosks. Be on the lookout for the ubiquitous red and yellow buses that may be seen cruising the city's streets.

- **Taxis:**

Taxis are widely available in Palma de Mallorca and are a practical method of transportation, particularly for quick trips or when you wish to get from point A to point B without making any stops. You may hail a cab on the street, and there are taxi stands all over the city. Make sure the taxi has a metre, and request a receipt when you reach your destination.

- **Bicycles:**

Palma is a bike-friendly city with many bike rental outlets and designated riding lanes. An enjoyable and environmentally friendly method to tour both the historic district and the beautiful coastal environs is by bicycle rental. You can simply pedal your way across the city thanks to the many hotels and hostels that also hire out bikes to visitors.

- **Car Rentals:**

Renting a car is a reasonable option if you want to explore the island beyond Palma. At the airport and in the city centre of Palma de Mallorca, a number of automobile rental agencies are present.

Remember that finding parking in the city might be difficult, so it's best to utilise public transport inside Palma.

- **Scooters and motorcycles:**

Both locals and tourists frequently travel on scooters and motorcycles. Rental options abound, and cycling across the city's congested streets is more convenient. If you intend to ride a scooter or motorcycle, make sure you have the required licences and insurance.

- **Walking:**

Palma's historic district is easy to navigate on foot and is both small and pedestrian-friendly. At your own leisure, meander around the cobblestone streets, find secret plazas, and take in the distinctive beauty of the city. For your urban travels, remember to wear cosy shoes.

- **Boat cruises and Ferries:**

Because Palma de Mallorca is an island location, you can take boat cruises and ferries to see the local coastline and smaller islands. These choices are excellent for day visits to secluded beaches, coves, and quaint coastal towns.

- **Trains:**

From Palma's Estació Intermodal, you can take a train to other sections of the island even if Palma itself doesn't have a robust train network. Train travel is a practical choice for discovering the picturesque countryside and other towns of Mallorca.

- **Tourist Trains and Trolleys:**

Taking a ride on a tourist train or tram is a fun and educational way to view the city's highlights. The most famous locations in Palma are traversed in these guided tours, which also offer historical and cultural insights.

Renting a Car or Bike

I. **Car Rental:**

Pros:

- **Flexibility:** In Palma de Mallorca, renting a car provides unmatched flexibility. You can plan your own trip, visit secluded beaches, and travel at your own speed through the picturesque countryside of the island.

- **Access to Remote Areas:** Mallorca is home to a large number of uninhabited coves, charming mountain communities, and natural parks. You can get to these off-the-beaten-path sites with a car, which might not be feasible using public transportation.

- **Convenience for Families or Groups:** Renting a car can be an affordable and practical way for a group of people to go around the island. This is especially true if you are travelling with family or friends.

- **Exploration at Your Leisure:** With a car, you have the freedom to go where you wish, take side trips, and spend more time at your favourite locations without worrying about finding a place to catch a ride.

Cons:

- **Parking Challenges:** Finding parking in Palma's city center can be challenging, especially during peak tourist season. Many hotels offer parking facilities, so consider booking accommodations that provide this service.

- **Traffic Congestion:** While the island generally has good roads, traffic congestion can occur in popular tourist areas, particularly during the summer months.
- **Costs:** Rental fees, fuel, and insurance can add up. Be sure to compare rental rates and understand the terms and conditions before booking.

II. Bike rental:

Pros:

- **Eco-Friendly:** Biking is a sustainable method to discover the city and its environs, in keeping with Palma's commitment to environmental preservation.
- **City Exploration Made Simple:** Biking is a great way to get around Palma's historic district because it is so small. Narrow streets are easily negotiated, and secret corners are easily found.
- **Healthy and Active:** Riding a bike is a great way to get out and explore the city while staying in shape and taking the time to appreciate the scenery.
- **Cost-effective:** hiring a bike is typically less expensive than hiring a car, and a lot of lodgings

either provide this service themselves or have agreements with rental companies.

Cons:

- **Limited Range:** While motorcycles are great for seeing cities, they might not be practical for travelling to far-flung or difficult-to-reach sections of the island.

- **Dependence on Weather:** The comfort of bicycling can be impacted by weather conditions like heat or rain. It's a good idea to look up the weather forecast before embarking on a bicycle trip.

- **Storage and Security:** Make sure your lodging has a secure place for you to store your bike when it's not in use, as bike theft can be a problem in some places.

Walking Tours:

Various Walking Tours

- **Tours of the Historic City Centre:** The Old Town (Casco Antiguo), or historic centre of Palma, is a maze of little streets, public spaces, and landmarks. You can learn about the city's fascinating history as you walk through the historic lanes and through architectural marvels like the Palma Cathedral (La Seu).

- **Cultural and artistic tours:** Palma is a centre for both. These trips concentrate on the city's galleries, museums, and other cultural establishments. The Es Baluard Museum features contemporary art, and lovely galleries feature the creations of regional artisans.

- **Gastronomic excursions:** Walking excursions that introduce you to Mallorcan cuisine are sure to please foodies. While learning about the island's culinary legacy, sample regional specialties in markets, tapas bars, and restaurants.

- **Market Tours:** Get a glimpse of Palma's bustling local markets, like Mercat de l'Olivar and Mercat de Santa Catalina. These excursions provide you the opportunity to engage with locals, sample fresh food, and browse souvenir shops.

- **Tours of Architecture:** Palma has a diverse range of buildings, from Gothic to Modernist. On specialised tours, see the city's architectural wonders, including as mediaeval palaces, modernist structures, and cutting-edge creations.

- **Nature and Scenic Tours:** Get away from the busy streets and discover Palma's natural splendour. Tours take you to verdant parks, gardens, and vantage locations where you can take in expansive city views, such Bellver Castle.

Advantages of Walking Tours include:

- **Local insights:** Well-informed guides offer historical context, first-hand accounts from the area, and insider knowledge to enhance your understanding of Palma's culture and history.
- **Hidden Gems:** Walking tours frequently take you to off-the-beaten-path locations you may otherwise miss, showing picturesque courtyards, hidden squares, and lesser-known landmarks.
- **Interaction:** Talk to locals, craftspeople, and merchants while on market and culinary tours to develop a stronger sense of cultural ties.

Walking tours allow you to experience the city while leaving the smallest possible carbon imprint.

They are also eco-friendly and support sustainable tourism.

- **Photographic Possibilities:** Palma's beauty is best experienced on foot, so you'll have lots of opportunity to take shots of charming streets, old buildings, and beautiful views.

Guidelines for a Wonderful Walking Tour Experience:

- Walking on cobblestone streets might be uneven, so wear comfortable shoes.
- In the sweltering summer months, wear clothing appropriate for the weather and carry drink and sunscreen.
- To guarantee a spot, reserve excursions well in advance, especially during the busiest travel period.
- Choose a tour that fits your interests and physical capabilities by looking at the duration of the journey.
- To get the most out of your guided experience, pay attention and inquire.

Yo Soy Mallorca

Yo Soy Mallorca (The Future)

Estació Intermodal

Bike Rentals

CHAPTER 4

Accommodation

Choosing the Right Accommodation

I. Location:

The first factor to take into account when selecting lodging in Palma de Mallorca is location. Consider the experiences that you want to have while visiting. Do you wish to be in the centre of the Old Town's historical district, close to restaurants and cultural attractions? Or would you rather stay at a hotel beside the beach and wake up to the sound of the waves? Take into account the area's accessibility to attractions, public transit, and the landscape you enjoy.

II. Type of Hotel:

From opulent resorts to affordable hostels, Palma provides a variety of lodging options. Here are a few possibilities:

- **Luxury Hotels and Resorts:** For a lavish experience, think about booking a room at one of the city's posh resorts or five-star hotels. Enjoy first-rate amenities, spa services, fine cuisine, and breathtaking sea views.

- **Boutiques Hotels:** Hotel boutiques in Palma de Mallorca are renowned for their distinctive appeal and individualised service. These more compact, privately owned buildings frequently have chic interior design and cosy settings.

- **Guesthouses and Bed & Breakfasts:** These lodging options are great if you're searching for a cosy, more affordable vacation. These places provide a welcoming atmosphere and a chance to meet local hosts.

- Short-term rentals are available in a variety of Palma apartments and villas on websites like Airbnb and Vrbo. This is the best choice if you want more room and the opportunity to prepare your own meals.

III.   Amenities and Facilities:

Take into account the perks that are most important to you. Swimming pools, on-site dining options, exercise centres, and spa services are all features of certain lodgings. Consider the amenities that will make your stay better, such as a rooftop patio with panoramic views or a cosy courtyard where you can unwind.

IV.   Budget and Rates:

To get the most for your money, set a budget for your lodging and compare prices. Remember that costs might change based on the time of year, so making reservations in advance or during off-peak times may result in discounts.

V.   Reviews and advice:

On websites like TripAdvisor or travel discussion groups, read reviews and ask for advice from other travellers. Making an informed decision can be aided by learning from other people's experiences.

VI.   Accessibility:

If you have special needs, take accessibility into account. For visitors with impairments, several lodgings offer accessible rooms and amenities.

VII.   Local Experiences:

Take into account lodgings that provide distinctive experiences if you want to fully immerse yourself in the local way of life. For instance, some boutique hotels offer culinary workshops, art exhibits, and local activities.

VIII.   Cancellation Policies:

Because travel is unpredictable, especially these days, it's a good idea to be aware of the cancellation policies of your preferred lodging in case your plans change.

Hotels and Resorts

I. **Castillo Hotel Son Vida:** This famous castle-turned-hotel gives a regal atmosphere and is perched on a hill overlooking Palma. It's a paradise for discriminating travellers, complete with a golf course, breathtaking views, and opulent amenities.

II. **Hotel Hospes Maricel & Spa:** This five-star boutique hotel is situated in the quaint coastal community of Cas Català and offers Mediterranean elegance, fine dining, and a tranquil spa.

III. **Nakar Hotel:** This Palma lodging option mixes contemporary style with comfort. A panorama of the city and the cathedral may be seen from its rooftop patio.

IV. **Iberostar Selection Playa de Palma:** Those looking to mix beach relaxation and city exploration would love this Playa de Palma beachfront hotel. It provides immediate access to the beach, a number of pools, and restaurants.

V. **Boutique lodging:**

- **Hotel Can Cera:** This boutique jewel is built in a 17th-century palace and is tucked away in Palma's historic district. It is well known for its cosy ambiance, attentive service, and stylish decor.

- **Palacio Ca Sa Galesa:** This Old Town treasure is a hidden gem that emanates old-world elegance. Additionally, the rooftop patio provides sweeping views of Palma's skyline. Each room is individually furnished.

VI. **Beachfront Hotels:**

- **Meliá Palma Bay:** Overlooking Palma Bay's glistening seas, this contemporary resort has chic accommodations, a rooftop pool, and quick access to the beach.

- Zafiro Palace Palmanova: This family-friendly resort is situated in Palmanova, just a short drive from Palma, and it offers a variety of pools, activities, and entertainment choices.

Budget-friendly lodgings:

- **Hostal Apuntadores:** Located in the centre of the Old Town, this inexpensive hostal provides easy access to the area's historical sites, eateries, and nightlife.

- **Hostal Ritzi:** For travellers on a budget, this inexpensive choice offers tidy and welcoming rooms close to the marina.

Hotels in the Regions Around:

- **St. Regis Mardavall Mallorca Resort:** This luxurious resort offers extravagance, breathtaking sea views, and access to local golf courses. It is located in the tranquil community of Costa d'en Blanes.

- **Sheraton Mallorca Arabella Golf Hotel:** Located in the upscale Arabella Golf complex, this resort provides golf aficionados with quick access to a variety of golf courses while being close to Palma.

All-Inclusive Options:

- **SENTIDO Cala Vias:** This all-inclusive resort is close to Palma and offers stunning sea views, a variety of eating options, and a tranquil atmosphere.

- **Grupotel Playa de Palma Suites & Spa:** Excellent choice for tourists seeking the ease of an all-inclusive vacation while nearby Palma's attractions.

Vacation Rentals:

I. **Vacation rental types:**

- **Apartments:** Palma has a wide selection of apartments, from comfortable studios in the centre of the Old Town to roomy penthouses with expansive sea views. These accommodations frequently have completely functional kitchens, so you may prepare your meals and savour regional cuisine.

- **Villas:** If you're travelling with a group of friends or a family, a villa offers roomy and private lodging. In Mallorca, there are several villas with private swimming pools, gardens, and other outdoor areas that are great for entertaining and socialising.

- **Homes on the beach:** Picture waking up to the sound of the ocean and having the beach right outside your door. In places like Playa de Palma and Cala Mayor, you can find beachfront vacation homes and villas.

- **Rural Retreats:** To get away from the rush and activity, stay in one of the charming farmhouses or cottages in Mallorca's tranquil countryside. These lodgings offer a peaceful setting for unwinding and taking in the island's scenic splendour.

Benefits of Vacation Rentals:

- Comforts of Home: With living rooms, bedrooms, kitchens, and frequently laundry facilities, vacation rentals offer a cosy atmosphere. As if it were your own house, you'll be able to unwind there with independence and space.

- Local Experience: Staying in a local area will give you a glimpse into Palma's everyday life. Shop at nearby markets, visit nearby cafés, and get involved in the neighbourhood.

- Cost Savings: Especially for larger parties or longer stays, vacation rentals are frequently more affordable than hotels. You can reduce your eating bills by learning to cook.

- Privacy and Space: Whether it's a private garden, deck, or pool, you'll have your own space to relax. No need to share facilities with other visitors.

- Flexible Dining: using a fully-equipped kitchen, you may cook your meals at home using local, fresh foods or eat out whenever you like.

Advice on Picking Vacation Rentals:

- Read reviews and conduct thorough research to choose a reliable rental. There are several choices available on websites like Airbnb, Vrbo, and Booking.com.

- Reserve Early: To guarantee your preferred dates and location, it's best to reserve your vacation rental well in advance, particularly during the busiest travel times.

- Verify Amenities: Make sure the rental offers the features you want, whether they be Wi-Fi, air conditioning, a pool, or a certain view.

- Interact with Hosts: Prior to making a reservation, get in touch with the property management or owner to clarify any details.

- Examine the Small Print: Read the rental agreement and cancellation policy to fully comprehend the terms and restrictions.

Hostels and Budget Options

I.   **Palma harbour Hostel - Albergue Juvenil:**

In the heart of the city, near to the harbour and the cathedral, is the laid-back Palma harbour Hostel - Albergue Juvenil. It includes individual and shared rooms, a common kitchen, a garden, and a terrace.

II.   **We Hostel Palma - Albergue Juvenil:**

This is another great choice, situated in the Old Town. It offers a range of room designs, including family rooms, private rooms, and dorm rooms.

The hostel also features a bar, a roof patio with city views, and a common kitchen.

III.   A chic hostel called **The Boc Hostels - Palma** is situated in the Santa Catalina district. It offers a range of lodging options, including private rooms, dorm rooms, and capsules. In addition, the hostel features a rooftop terrace, a game area, and a communal kitchen.

IV. In the Son Armadams district, **Urban Hostel Palma** is a less expensive choice. It provides individual and shared rooms, a common kitchen, and a common room.

V. About 15 kilometres from Palma, in the municipality of Esporles, is the **Hostel Fleming Albergue Juvenil.** It has individual and communal rooms, a kitchen that is shared, and a garden.

Top Accommodation Picks

I. Boutique Luxury at Sant Francesc Hotel Singular:

- **Location:** This five-star boutique hotel is set in a 19th-century townhouse and is located in the centre of the Old Town.

- **Highlights:** include the elegant architecture, the serene courtyard, the Michelin-starred Quadrat Restaurant & Garden, and the rooftop terrace with its breathtaking views.

- **Why Stay:** To experience a unique fusion of history, luxury, and individualised service in a premier setting.

II. **Beachfront Bliss at Iberostar Selection Playa de Palma:**

- Location: Just a short drive from the city centre, near Playa de Palma's seafront.

- **Highlights:** include easy access to the beach, numerous pools, a spa, and a selection of restaurants.

- **Why Stay:** Perfect for beach lovers looking for a tranquil resort experience with quick access to the beach and the attractions of Palma.

III. **Urban Elegance at Hotel Nakar:**

- **Location:** In the centre of Palma, close to the city's gastronomic and cultural districts.

- Highlights include a contemporary style, a rooftop terrace with a pool, a restaurant on the top floor, and chic rooms.

- **Why Stay:** Ideal for those who want to walk through Palma's bustling city centre and historic landmarks.

IV. **Coastal Serenity at Hipotels Gran Playa de Palma:**

- **Location:** A short drive from the city and only a few metres from Playa de Palma beach.

- Highlights include a tranquil spa, indoor and outdoor swimming pools, and cosy accommodations with views of the ocean.

- **Why Stay:** Perfect for beach lovers seeking a tranquil hideaway with quick access to Palma.

V. **Historic Elegance at Hotel Can Cera:**

- **Location:** Tucked away in the heart of Palma's old town, close to important sites like the cathedral.

- Highlights include a 17th-century palace with uniquely built apartments, a courtyard, and a romantic ambiance.

- **Why Stay:** For a pleasant and secluded stay among the city's ancient gems.

VI. **Seaside Luxury at Hospes Maricel & Spa:**

- Located not far from Palma in the coastal community of Cas Català.

- Highlights include a spa, superb restaurants, seaside views, and Mediterranean elegance.

- **Why Stay:** Ideal for a calm retreat or a romantic break with beautiful views.

VII.   **Budget-Friendly Comfort at Hostal Apuntadores:**

- **Location:** Situated close to dining options and nightlife in Palma's Old Town.
- Highlights include affordable prices, convenient location, and cosy accommodations.
- **Why Stay:** Perfect for travellers on a tight budget who want to be near the city's attractions.

VIII.   **Countryside Charm at FincaHotel Can Coll:**

- **Location:** A short drive from Palma, tucked away in the Mallorcan countryside.
- Highlights include peaceful settings, a pool, and a kind greeting.

Why Stay: To enjoy a tranquil escape in the calm landscape of the island.

CHAPTER 5

Exploring Palma de Mallorca

This dynamic capital city is a hidden gem of experiences just waiting to be discovered. It is surrounded by the crystalline waves of the Mediterranean. Palma de Mallorca offers a mesmerising experience that is sure to leave a lasting impression on every visitor, from its mediaeval Old Town steeped in centuries' worth of tales to the immaculate beaches that line its coastline.

As soon as you step into the Old Town's cobblestone streets, you'll be taken back in time as you stroll among Gothic buildings, secret courtyards, and charming squares. The majestic Palma Cathedral (La Seu), a marvel of Gothic architecture, bears witness to the city's illustrious history. Investigate its fascinating interior and awe at the dance of light and shadow.

Palma's cultural fabric is knitted together with music, art, and a positive outlook on life. Wander through the maze-like streets, where artisanal studios and shops highlight regional ingenuity. At lively markets and welcoming tapas bars, pause to enjoy the flavours of Mallorcan food. The city's culinary scene is proof of its dedication to authenticity and use of local, fresh ingredients.

However, Palma de Mallorca extends beyond the city limits. You can find a world of natural wonders if you venture outside the municipal limits.

Sand-filled bays and towering cliffs are encircled by crystal-clear waters, creating the perfect setting for water sports activities and days spent in the sun. Explore the verdant countryside, which is painted in a palette of greens and golds by vineyards, olive groves, and almond orchards.

Old Town (La Seu)

A Glimpse into History: La Seu, which has Roman origins, is a living reminder of Mallorca's past. The Palma Cathedral, the city's most well-known structure, is a magnificent example of Gothic design. Officially known as the **"Cathedral-Basilica of Santa Maria of Palma,"** this magnificent building is a colossal testimony to the island's enduring religious tradition and rich artistic legacy. The church draws your attention as you get closer because of its towering spires and elaborate façade, which hint to an equally attractive inside.

Exploring the Cathedral: When you enter the Palma Cathedral, you're met with a calm, spacious setting decorated with elaborate chapels, exquisite stained glass, and a sense of awe that permeates the air. As sunlight pours through its intricate decorations, the rose window of the cathedral, also referred to as the "Eye of God," bathes the inside in a kaleidoscope of colours.

The Royal Palace of **La Almudaina** is a mediaeval fortification that has been used by kings and monarchs as a palace. It is located next to the cathedral. Its beautifully restored chambers and courtyards offer a window into royal life throughout history. You'll be taken back in time to a time when Mallorca was a prosperous monarchy as you walk through its halls.

Cobbled lanes and Hidden Courtyards:

Beyond the cathedral and palace, Old Town's winding lanes encourage investigation. Cobbled streets wind through the neighbourhood, exposing secret courtyards, adorable squares, and lovely facades.

Every turn you make offers the promise of a secret treasure just waiting to be found.

Shopping and Dining:

The dining and shopping districts of Old Town are both thriving. Discover local craft shops, art galleries, and quaint boutiques. Eat typical Mallorcan fare in local bars when you're hungry, or eat outside in charming squares.

Local activities & Festivals:

Festivals and cultural activities keep La Seu vibrant all year long. The neighbourhood embraces Mallorca's cultural past with colourful events like Sant Sebastià and religious processions during Holy Week.

A Timeless Atmosphere:

Palma de Mallorca's Old Town (La Seu) is more than just a historic area; it is a live, breathing example of the island's eternal legacy. A monument to the ongoing allure of this magnificent part of Mallorca, its old stones resound with the footsteps of centuries of tourists, and its dynamic current. A trip through La Seu promises to be an enthralling excursion back in time, whether you're a history buff, an architecture aficionado, or just a traveller looking for real experiences.

Bellver Castle

- **A Remarkable Architectural Gem:**

Bellver Castle, or **"Castell de Bellver"** in Catalan, is famed for its peculiar circular design, a rarity among mediaeval defences. Bellver Castle is a remarkable architectural gem. This architectural gem from the 14th century is one of the very few examples of its kind in all of Europe and the only one f its kind in Spain.

History and Origins:

Bellver Castle was built in the early 14th century at the request of King James II of Mallorca as a royal residence and defensive castle. Its clever hilltop positioning offered protection as well as a vantage point from which to keep an eye on the city and the nearby seas.

Circular Perfection:

Bellver Castle's round design is among its most alluring characteristics. Its distinctive and well-coordinated aspect is provided by the castle's imposing defensive walls, which enclose a central courtyard. As no single spot within the castle's walls is necessarily superior to another, the circular design stands for equality and harmony.

The Interior:

A wonderful historical experience awaits you if you go inside Bellver Castle. A museum that explores the history of Mallorca and the castle is housed there. Discover the gothic-style halls, adore the exquisitely restored royal rooms, and climb to the rooftop terrace for spectacular panoramic views of Palma, the ocean, and the Tramuntana Mountains.

Events & Cultural Delight:

Bellver Castle is a thriving centre of culture, not just a historical artefact. It holds a range of activities all year long, including traditional festivals as well as concerts and exhibitions. The Festival of Sant Joan, which takes place on June 23rd and features a stunning fireworks display with the castle as the backdrop, is one of the most well-known occasions.

A Natural Oasis

The Bellver Woods (Bosque de Bellver), a verdant wooded region, surround Bellver Castle. This serene park has covered pathways for leisurely strolls, making it the ideal place to get away from the bustle of the city.

Experience for Visitors:

From Palma, Bellver Castle is simply reachable via a short drive or a delightful walk. Its distinctive architecture and panoramic views make it a must-visit location for history aficionados, architecture lovers, and anybody looking to immerse themselves in Mallorca's past.

Palma's Beaches:

- **Playa de Palma:**

This is the most well-known beach in Palma de Mallorca, and is only a short stroll from the city centre. Families will find it to be the perfect beach because of its length and calm seas.

Along the beach, there are many eateries, bars, and facilities for participating in water sports. Sunbed and umbrella costs range from €15 to €20 per day.

- **Platja de Palma:**

This is a tiny beach near to Playa de Palma. It is less congested and more laid back. This beach has less amenities as well, but it is still a fantastic choice for swimming and tanning. Sunbed and umbrella costs range from €10 to €15 per day.

- **Cala Major:**

This protected cove may be found not far from Palma de Mallorca. It is a well-liked family beach with calm waters. The beach is less developed than Playa de Palma, however there are a few restaurants and bars there. Sunbeds and umbrellas cost between €12 and €18 per day.

- **Cala Fornells:**

Small cove Cala Fornells is situated northwest of Palma de Mallorca. The beach has crystal-clear seas and is less busy. The beach is more isolated than Playa de Palma, however it does have a few restaurants and bars nearby. Sunbeds and umbrellas cost between €10 and €15 per day.

- **Cala Deia:**

It's a beautiful cove west of Palma de Mallorca. It's a well-liked swimming and snorkelling beach. Although there are a few bars and restaurants along the beach, it is more pricey than Playa de Palma. Sunbed and umbrella costs range from €15 to €20 per day.

- **Cala Sa Conca:**

Southwest of Palma de Mallorca is a little cove known as Cala Sa Conca. It is a remote beach with pristine water. This beach is a terrific location to unwind and appreciate the peace and quiet even though there are no restaurants or bars there

- **Cala Llombards:**

Southwest of Palma de Mallorca is a gorgeous cove called Cala Llombards. It is a well-liked beach for swimming and tanning. Although there are a few eateries and pubs nearby, the beach is still rather undeveloped.

- **Cala d'Or:**

This Mallorcan town in the southeast has a number of coves. Despite being a well-liked tourist attraction, the beaches are nevertheless quite uncrowded. Sunbed and umbrella costs range from €10 to €15 per day.

- **Es Trenc:**

A lengthy sandy beach that can be found in Mallorca's southeast. It is a well-liked swimming and tanning beach. This beach is a terrific spot to unwind and take in the local natural beauty even though there are no restaurants or bars there.

- **Formentor:**

Northeast of Mallorca is home to the lovely peninsula known as Formentor. It boasts a number of beaches, notably Cala Formentor, one of Mallorca's busiest beaches. Sunbeds and umbrellas cost between €15 and €20 per day.

Please be aware that these costs are just intended to serve as a basic guide and may change depending on the season, the particular beach, and the sunbed or umbrella type you select.

In addition, bear the following in mind when picking a beach in Palma de Mallorca:

The time of year: The summer months (June to September) are the busiest on the beaches. Try going to the beach in the winter (November to March) or the shoulder seasons (May and October) if you want a more laid-back experience.

The kind of beach: Some beaches are excellent for water activities or sunbathing, while others are better for swimming. When selecting a beach, take your hobbies into account.

The amenities: Different beaches have different numbers of amenities like restaurants, bars, and rentals for water activities. Make careful to pick a beach that has been developed if you want one with lots of amenities.

The cost: The cost of beaches can range from free to pricey. Make sure to pick an economical beach if you're on a tight budget.

Palma Aquarium

A World of Aquatic Wonders:

The goal of Palma Aquarium is to open a window into the various marine habitats that may be found in the Mediterranean Sea and other oceans around the world. The aquarium accomplishes this by showcasing the intricacy and beauty of undersea life in a number of breathtaking exhibits.

Major highlights

The Big Blue:

This large tank, which serves as the centrepiece of Palma Aquarium, provides a close-up view of the marine life in the Mediterranean. A mesmerising spectacle may be seen as schools of vibrant fish, graceful rays, and majestic sharks glide across the transparent waters.

Beyond the tanks, Palma Aquarium has lovely Mediterranean gardens. Visitors can unwind and discover more about the local flora in these exquisitely planted places.

Without leaving Mallorca, enter the heart of the Amazon Rainforest: An Amazon Adventure. This exhibit features unusual animals in a lush rainforest setting, including piranhas, turtles, and iguanas.

Experiential Learning:

Education and conservation are given a lot of weight at Palma Aquarium. Visitors can take part in interactive events, workshops, and guided tours that give them information about marine life and conservation efforts.

Conservation Initiatives:

The aquarium actively participates in marine conservation initiatives, such as research, rehabilitation, and campaigns to spread awareness of the value of safeguarding our seas.

Family-Friendly Experience:

Palma Aquarium is a place that is welcoming to people of all families and to kids of all ages. Children's imaginations are captured by the exhibits, and interactive spaces let them interact with and get up close to marine life. Every visit to the aquarium is a worthwhile experience thanks to its dedication to education.

Visitor Information:

- **Location:** Palma Aquarium is located in Can Pastilla, which is conveniently close to the city centre of Palma de Mallorca and reachable by public transportation.
- **Opening Hours:** The aquarium normally is open all year round, with different hours according on the season. For the most recent details on admission

costs and operating hours, it is advised to visit the official website.

- **Accessibility:** Palma Aquarium is equipped to accommodate visitors with a range of requirements, including wheelchair accessibility.

- **A Trip into the Depths:** Palma Aquarium cordially welcomes you to take an enthralling trip into the Mediterranean Sea's and other abyssal depths.

This underwater oasis promises a memorable experience that showcases the beauty and significance of our planet's seas, whether you're a marine enthusiast, a family wanting an educational adventure, or simply seeking a moment of wonder.

Museums and Art Galleries

- **Palma Cathedral Museum (Museu Diocesà):**

Highlights: This museum displays religious artwork, sculptures, and artefacts and is located inside the magnificent Palma Cathedral. It is a special chance to discover the cathedral's past and architectural nuances while appreciating its artistic treasures.

- **Es Baluard Museum of Modern and Contemporary Art:**

Highlights: Es Baluard is a modern art gallery with a view of Palma's harbour. From paintings and sculptures to multimedia installations, it showcases a varied array of works by regional and worldwide artists. The rooftop terrace of the museum provides expansive views of both the city and the ocean.

- **Fundació Pilar i Joan Miró:**

Highlights: This foundation exhibits the paintings, sculptures, and graphic works of the renowned Spanish artist Joan Miró. Visitors can look into Miró's creative process and learn about how his art has developed.

- **Palau March Museum (Museu Palau March):**

Highlights: This museum is housed in a stunning estate and features an interesting collection of sculptures, pottery, and paintings. Famous artists' sculptures can be seen in the museum's magnificent grounds.

- **Royal Palace of La Almudaina (Palacio Real de La Almudaina):**

Highlights: Although the palace is largely a historical landmark, it also accommodates transient art exhibitions, offering a distinctive setting for contemporary art against a backdrop of mediaeval architecture.

- **Mallorca Museum:**

Highlights: With archaeological artefacts, works of art, and ethnographic collections that shed light on Mallorca's past, this museum provides a thorough picture of the island's history and culture.

- **Casal Solleric:**

Highlights: Casal Solleric, which is housed in a gorgeously renovated estate, features contemporary art shows that feature the creations of both up-and-coming and seasoned artists. Even the environment is a piece of art.

- **Can Prunera Museum of Modernism:**

Highlights: This museum honours the art and architecture of the modernist movement and is located in the charming village of Sóller, not far from Palma. There are pieces in its collection by well-known artists including Picasso and Klimt.

- **Juan March Foundation (Fundació Joan March):**

Highlights: This foundation offers transient exhibitions of modern art, frequently including pieces by highly regarded artists from around the world. It's a vibrant setting that encourages innovation and creative inquiry.

Visitor Information:

- It's best to check museums and galleries' official websites or get in touch with them personally for the most recent information as opening times, entrance prices, and exhibition schedules may differ among them.
- In order to provide visitors a fuller understanding of its collections and exhibitions, several cultural institutions offer guided tours and educational programmes.

Parks and Gardens

- **Parc de la Mar:**

Location: This park, which gives stunning views of both the cathedral and the sea, is tucked away at the foot of Palma's famous Cathedral (La Seu). It's a peaceful area where you may unwind and see the splendour of the city's old town.

- **Jardí de ses Estacions (Station Gardens):**

Location: This garden is a tranquil haven in the midst of the bustle of transport hubs because it is located close to the main train and bus stations. It's a fantastic location for a calm stroll or some quiet time.

- **Parc de Sa Riera:**

Location: With play areas, ponds, and shady walkways, this park is a refuge for urban dwellers. Families and locals frequently picnic there and engage in other outdoor pursuits.

- **Sa Feixina Park:**

Sa Feixina is a historical park with statues, fountains, and terraced gardens. It's a beautiful area to stroll lazily while taking in the urban vegetation of the city.

- **Parc de la Feixina:**

Location: This more recent park is next to Sa Feixina Park and has contemporary sculptures, a sizable playground, and open areas for relaxing. Locals and travellers looking for a tranquil escape frequently frequent this location.

- **Passeig de Sagrera (Sagrera Promenade):**

Location: This lovely promenade offers a pleasant path for strolling, jogging, or just taking in the sea vistas and fresh air. It stretches along Palma's waterfront. Sunset is quite gorgeous.

- **Gardens of S'Hort del Rei:**

Location: These beautifully designed gardens, which are close to the Almudaina Palace and the Cathedral, offer a tranquil setting with fountains, orange trees, and breathtaking views of the old structures.

- **Parc de la Marquesa:**

Location: This park is a nice green space with play areas, a pond, and a lot of shady locations to unwind. It is situated in the hip Santa Catalina neighbourhood.

- **Parc de la Quinta Alegre:**

Located in the El Terreno neighbourhood, this park provides a tranquil haven with strolling pathways and benches. It's a peaceful getaway where you may relax amidst the outdoors.

- **Parc de la Freginal:**

Location: This park, which is close to Portixol, has a boardwalk that runs down the shoreline, making it a great place for a bike ride or a stroll along the shore.

Cathedral-Basilica of Santa Maria of Palma (La Seu)

Bellver Castle

Palma's Beach

Palma Aquarium

Palma Nightlife

CHAPTER 6

Dining and Nightlife

A. Mallorcan Cuisine:

Get a taste of the cuisine by trying dishes like "ensaimada," "paella," and "sobrassada," a spicy sausage spread. For a genuine experience of Mallorca, visit traditional eateries called "cellers."

B. Seafood Extravaganza:

Palma has a lot of seafood eateries because to its coastal setting. Enjoy the freshest catches of the day, such as 'gambas al ajillo' (garlic prawns) and 'calamari a la plancha' (grilled squid).

C. Market Magic:

Visit the city's busy market, Mercat de l'Olivar, to enjoy the tapas, cheeses, and produce that are grown nearby. You may enjoy flavours from all throughout Spain in this culinary haven.

D. International Fusion:

Palma's eclectic food scene exhibits an international flair. Explore trendy eateries that serve fusion food, including sushi and Mediterranean-Middle Eastern fusion.

E. Dining on the Roof:

Select one of the city's rooftop eateries to enhance your eating experience. As you savour fine dining outside under the stars, take in the breathtaking views of Palma.

Nightlife Extravaganza:

The nightlife scene in Palma de Mallorca typically begins later, with many establishments becoming busier after midnight.

Before going out, it's a good idea to examine the criteria of particular clubs and bars because dress regulations vary.

Remind yourself to drink sensibly and stay hydrated, especially during the hot summer nights.

I.   Paseo Marítimo:

The hub of Palma's nightlife is this coastal promenade. You may dance the night away in the bars, clubs and lounges that line the street. It's a must to visit places like Tito's and Pacha Mallorca.

II.   La Lonja:

After sundown, the old La Lonja neighbourhood comes alive with nightlife. In this charming neighbourhood, take advantage of the cocktails, live music, and energetic environment.

III.   Jazz and Live Music:

Palma has jazz clubs and live music places where you may listen to soulful music in a cosy environment if you want a more relaxed evening.

IV.   Tapas and Wine Bars:

Explore the lovely wineries and tapas bars in the city. Try some regional wines and savour a selection of tapas delicacies, such as "patatas bravas" and "croquetas."

V.   Late-Nite Beach Parties:

In the summer, beachfront clubs like Nikki Beach and Nassau Beach Club throw amazing beach parties that go till the wee hours.

VI. Cultural Evenings:

Attend performances in the Auditorium de Palma or the Teatre Principal for a cultured evening out, where you can see theatre, ballet, and music.

Traditional Mallorcan Cuisine

I. **Ensaimada:**

This is a sweet pastry made with yeast dough and filled with whipped cream or custard. It is the most famous pastry in Mallorca and is often served as a dessert or snack. Prices range from €1.50 to €3.00 for a small ensaimada, and €3.00 to €5.00 for a large ensaimada.

II. **Coca de trampó:**

This is a tomato and onion salad that is typically served as a tapa or starter. It is made with tomatoes, onions, garlic, olive oil, and salt. Prices range from €2.00 to €4.00 for a small coca de trampó, and €4.00 to €6.00 for a large coca de trampó.

III.   **Arròs brut:**

A rice-based stew with meat, fish, veggies, and seasonings. It's a filling dish that's frequently offered as the main course. A slice of arr's brut costs between €15.00 and €20.00.

IV.   **Llom amb col:**

This recipe calls for stewing pig loin in tomato sauce while it is wrapped in cabbage leaves. It's a classic winter dish that's frequently served with potatoes. A slice of llom amb col costs between €12.00 and €15.00.

V.   **Frito mallorquí:**

This meal is often served as a tapa or beginning and is composed of fried seafood and vegetables. Squid, prawns, octopus, and vegetables including potatoes, peppers, and onions are used to make it. For a serving of frito mallorqu, prices range from €6 to €10.

VI.   **Sobrasada:**

Made from pork, paprika and garlic, this hot sausage is a Spanish delicacy. It is sometimes offered as a tapa or a component of other recipes like coca de trampó. A slice of sobrasada costs between €2.00 and €4.00.

VII. **Panades:**

These are savoury pies with cheese, cheese or meat within. Despite being a classic Easter dish, they are suitable for year-round consumption. The cost of a panade is between €2.50 and €4.00.

VIII. **Tumbet:** T

his vegetable stew has eggplant, potatoes, tomatoes, peppers, and onions. A common summertime entrée, it is frequently served with grilled fish or pork. For a part of Tumblr, prices range from €10.00 to €15.00.

IX. **Bunyols:**

These are sugar-coated, delicious doughnuts that are frequently fried. They are a well-liked dessert or snack, particularly around the holidays. A portion of bunyols costs between €1.50 and €3.00.

X. **Leche merengada:**

This traditional Mallorcan beverage is created from cinnamon, sugar, and milk. During the winter, it is a common way to warm up and is frequently served hot. For a glass of leche merengada, prices range from €2 to €4.

Best Restaurants and Cafes

Restaurants:

I.   **Marc Fosh:** This Michelin-starred restaurant, led by chef Marc Fosh, offers a modern Mediterranean dining experience. The seasonal tasting menus feature locally sourced ingredients prepared with inventive flair.

II.   **Celler Sa Premsa:** A beloved Mallorcan institution, Celler Sa Premsa is known for its rustic atmosphere and traditional island dishes. Try the "tumbet" and "frito Mallorquín" for an authentic taste of Mallorca.

III.   **Aromata:** Chef Andreu Genestra combines Mallorcan ingredients with innovative techniques at Aromata. The result is a creative menu that pays homage to the island's culinary heritage.

IV.   **Adrian Quetglas:** Enjoy a culinary journey that blends Mallorcan and international flavors at Adrian Quetglas. The restaurant's stylish ambiance and meticulously crafted dishes make for a memorable dining experience.

V.   **Canela:** Located in the trendy Santa Catalina neighborhood, Canela offers a fusion of

Mediterranean and Asian cuisines. Their sushi and seafood dishes are particularly renowned.

VI. **Can Eduardo:** This iconic seafood restaurant overlooking Palma's marina serves up fresh catches of the day, offering a quintessential Mediterranean dining experience.

VII. **La Mémé:** A hidden gem, La Mémé is a cozy restaurant known for its exceptional service and delicious French-Mediterranean cuisine. The chef's tasting menu is a delightful surprise.

Cafes:

I. **Ca'n Joan de S'Aigo:** Established in 1700, this historic cafe is famous for its traditional pastries, "ensaimadas," and delightful hot chocolate. It's a step back in time.

II. **Rialto Living Café:** Located within the stylish Rialto Living concept store, this cafe offers a tranquil oasis where you can enjoy gourmet sandwiches, pastries, and a selection of teas and coffees.

III. **La Finca Café:** Situated in a charming garden setting, La Finca Café is a picturesque spot for brunch or a coffee break. They serve a variety of healthy dishes and artisanal coffee.

IV. **Rosevelvet Bakery:** If you have a sweet tooth, Rosevelvet Bakery is a must-visit. Indulge in their delectable cupcakes, brownies, and other homemade treats in a cozy atmosphere.

V. **Mama Carmen Café:** Tucked away in the historic center, Mama Carmen Café is known for its artisanal coffee and welcoming ambiance. It's perfect to relax after exploring the city.

VI. **Ca'n Joan de S'Aigo:** Established in 1700, this historic cafe is famous for its traditional pastries, "ensaimadas," and delightful hot chocolate. It's a step back in time.

VII. **Rialto Living Café:** Located within the stylish Rialto Living concept store, this cafe offers a tranquil oasis where you can enjoy gourmet sandwiches, pastries, and a selection of teas and coffees.

VIII. **La Finca Café:** Situated in a charming garden setting, La Finca Café is a picturesque spot for brunch or a coffee break. They serve a variety of healthy dishes and artisanal coffee.

IX. **Rosevelvet Bakery:** If you have a sweet tooth, Rosevelvet Bakery is a must-visit. Indulge in their delectable cupcakes, brownies, and other homemade treats in a cozy atmosphere.

X. **Mama Carmen Café:** Tucked away in the historic center, Mama Carmen Café is known for its artisanal coffee and welcoming ambiance. It's a perfect spot to relax after exploring the city.

Budget-Friendly Restaurants:

I. **Cafè Sóller:** Located near the central train station, Cafè Sóller offers a menu of Mallorcan and Mediterranean dishes at reasonable prices. Their daily specials are particularly rich value.

II. **Casa Alvaro:** This cozy restaurant in the La Lonja neighborhood is known for its authentic Spanish tapas. Order a variety of small plates to share, and you'll enjoy a satisfying meal without breaking the bank.

III. **Can Joan de S'Aigo:** While famous for its traditional pastries, this historic cafe also offers savory options like sandwiches and salads at budget-friendly prices. Don't forget to try their renowned hot chocolate.

IV. **Bar Bosch:** Located in the heart of Palma's historic center, Bar Bosch has been serving locals and visitors since 1936. They offer a selection of sandwiches, including their famous "lomo con col" (pork loin with cabbage).

V. **Celler Sa Premsa:** This classic Mallorcan restaurant is known for its traditional cuisine. They have an affordable daily menu that includes local specialties like "frito Mallorquín" and "tumbet."

Budget-Friendly Cafes:

I. **Mama Carmen Café:** Tucked away in the historic center, this cozy cafe is a great spot for a budget-friendly coffee break. They also offer a selection of pastries and light snacks.

II. **Café Ca'n Toni:** Located in the charming Sa Gerreria neighborhood, Café Ca'n Toni serves affordable breakfast options, including sandwiches and croissants, making it a perfect place to start your day.

III. **Café L'Antiquari:** This artsy cafe is a hidden gem in Palma's La Lonja district. You can enjoy coffee, fresh juices, and sandwiches in a relaxed atmosphere.

IV. **Café de Oriente:** Situated near Palma's cathedral, this cafe offers a range of coffees, teas, and pastries at budget-friendly prices. The outdoor seating section is perfect for people-watching.

V. **Can Joan de S'Aigo:** While famous for its traditional pastries, this historic cafe also offers savory options like sandwiches and salads at budget-friendly prices. Don't forget to try their renowned hot chocolate.

VI. **Bar Bosch:** Located in the heart of Palma's historic center, Bar Bosch has been serving locals and visitors since 1936. They offer a selection of sandwiches, including their famous "lomo con col" (pork loin with cabbage).

VII. **Celler Sa Premsa:** This classic Mallorcan restaurant is known for its traditional cuisine. They have an affordable daily menu that includes local specialties like "frito Mallorquín" and "tumbet."

Tapas Bars and Local Eateries

I. Tapas Neighborhoods:

Santa Catalina: With various bars and eateries serving a wide selection of small plates, this hip neighbourhood is a tapas destination. Discover hidden treasures by navigating the city.

II. La Lonja:

The lovely tapas bars and neighbourhood restaurants may be found in the storied La Lonja neighbourhood. It's the perfect place to savour authentic Spanish cuisine.

III. Mercat de l'Olivar:

This vibrant market in the centre of Palma is not only a haven for foodies, but it is also a location where you can discover tapas stands selling seasonal and fresh snacks.

Tapas Bars:

I. Cerveceria La Lonja:

This popular tapas joint in La Lonja is renowned for its welcoming ambiance and an extensive menu of tapas. Don't forget to try the "pulpo a la gallega" (octopus in Galician style).

II. Tast Club:

Located in the city's centre, Tast Club serves inventive tapas compositions influenced by Spanish and Mallorcan traditions. It combines innovation and heritage.

III. Bar España:

Both residents and visitors love this old tavern on the Plaça Major. The perfect place to sample traditional Spanish tapas like "albondigas" (meatballs) and "patatas bravas" is here.

IV. Taberna La Boveda:

This quaint tapas tavern is built in a 17th-century structure and is close to the cathedral. A variety of tapas, including regional delicacies, are available.

V. Can Joan de S'Aigo:

This old café is well-known for its pastries and hot chocolate, but it also serves savoury tapas like "cocas" (flatbreads) with toppings like "tumbet" and "sobrassada."

Local Eateries:

I. Casa Alvaro:

Casa Alvaro is a quaint restaurant in La Lonja that provides traditional Mallorcan cuisine and real Spanish tapas. You should definitely try the "tumbet" and the "frito Mallorquin" there.

II. Bar Dia:

This laid-back neighbourhood restaurant, which is close to the Mercat de l'Olivar, serves up fresh seafood and typical Mallorcan meals. The "arroz brut" they serve is excellent.

I. Es Rebost:

A restaurant devoted to upholding and developing Mallorcan culinary customs, Es Rebost serves up specialties like "sopes Mallorquines" and "coca de trampó."

II. Celler Sa Premsa:

This venerable establishment serves traditional Mallorcan cuisine. Visit to experience authentic Mallorcan cuisine, such as "paella" and "tumbet."

III. Bar Bosch:

A venerable restaurant in the Plaça Rei Joan Carles I, Bar Bosch is renowned for its traditional Spanish cuisine and traditional tapas.

IV. Es Brollador:

Located in the Santa Catalina district, this family-run eatery serves up tapas and meals from Mallorca in a warm environment.

Vegetarian and Vegan Options

Veggie Restaurants:

I. Bon Lloc:

For years, diners have enjoyed this renowned vegetarian restaurant in Palma. They use ingredients from the local area to create a variety of inventive and delectable dishes on their menu.

II. EcoCenter:

EcoCenter is a vegetarian and vegan restaurant with a large menu that includes items like vegetable burgers, wraps, and healthy salads. It is situated in the Santa Catalina neighbourhood.

Vegan-Friendly Eateries:

I.   Raima Green:

Located close to the city's centre, Raima Green is renowned for its inventive plant-based cuisine and vegan tapas. Everything from vegan "croquetas" to sushi rolls can be found on the menu.

II.   Ziva To Go:

Ziva To Go is a vegan cafe serving a variety of vegan foods, such as salads, sandwiches, smoothie bowls, and desserts. It is situated in the hip Santa Catalina neighbourhood.

I.   Indian food:

Vegetarian and vegan alternatives such vegetable curries, lentil meals, and naan bread are available at various Indian restaurants in Palma.

II.   **Asian Cuisine:**

Vegetarian stir-fries, sushi rolls, and meals made with tofu are available at many Asian restaurants in Palma, particularly Thai and Japanese eateries.

III.   **Cafes and Bakeries:**

Rosevelvet Bakery: This establishment, which is well-known for its sweets, also provides vegan cupcakes, brownies, and cookies.

IV.   **Café 4 Deli:**

This eatery, which is close to the Mercat de l'Olivar, offers vegan sandwiches, salads, and fresh juices for breakfast and lunch.

Market Visits:

I.   **Mercat de l'Olivar:**

While mostly a fresh food market, Mercat de l'Olivar also has a number of food kiosks where you can find fresh fruits, vegetables, and ingredients for your own vegetarian or vegan dishes.

II.   Customizable Menus:

In many Palma restaurants, food can be changed to suit vegetarian or vegan preferences. You are welcome to request menu suggestions or changes from your server.

III.   Supermarkets and Health Food Stores:

You may stock up on vegetarian and vegan goods, such as plant-based meat substitutes, dairy-free options, and organic fruit, in Palma's numerous supermarkets and health food outlets.

Palma's Nightlife Scene

Tips for Nightlife in Palma:

- The nightlife in Palma typically begins later, with many establishments becoming busier after midnight.
- Before going out, it's a good idea to examine the criteria of particular clubs and bars because dress regulations vary.
- Remind yourself to drink sensibly and stay hydrated, especially during the hot summer nights.

I. Paseo Marítimo:

Tito's: This renowned nightclub has long been a mainstay of Paseo Maritimo. Tito's provides an incredible night of electronic music and dancing into the early hours thanks to its numerous floors and dance spaces.

II. Pacha Mallorca:

This club, which is a part of the renowned Pacha franchise, has top-notch DJs, themed events, and a glitzy ambiance. The marina can be seen from the outdoor patio, which makes a stunning backdrop for a dancing night.

III. La Lonja:

- **Mar de Nudos:** A sophisticated atmosphere for savouring beautifully made cocktails and tapas can be found at Mar de Nudos, a contemporary cocktail bar located in the centre of La Lonja. It's ideal for giving your evening a dash of class.

- **Blue Jazz Club:** Perched atop the Saratoga Hotel, this jazz venue provides excellent drinks, live music, and sweeping panoramas of Palma's cityscape. It's a chic location for a relaxing evening of jazz.

IV.   Santa Catalina:

Hostal Cuba Sky Bar: Hostal Cuba Sky Bar is a bar with breathtaking views of the city and the ocean that is perched on the hotel's rooftop. Before the nightlife starts, take in the sunset while sipping on a variety of beverages.

- **Jimmy's Bar:** A welcoming pub in Santa Catalina, Jimmy's Bar is renowned for its live music and welcoming ambiance. It's a nice spot for relaxing with a cold beer and enjoyable music.

V.   Carrer de Blanquerna:

- **Café Árbol:** This well-liked establishment in the Blanquerna neighbourhood features live music events and a relaxed atmosphere. Because of the laid-back atmosphere, both residents and tourists love it.

VI.   Beachfront Clubs:

- **Nikki Beach:** In the summer, Nikki Beach is transformed into a glitzy beach club with live DJs, beachside relaxation, and energetic events that last well into the night.

- **Nassau Beach Club:** On Playa de Palma, the Nassau Beach Club provides a laid-back beachside ambience by day before transforming into a lively club with DJs and dancing at night.

VII.   **Cultural Experiences:**

Teatre Principal: For a more cultured night out, check out performances in the Auditorium de Palma and Teatre Principal, which present theatre, ballet, concerts and other events.

VIII.   Local Bars and Tapas Joints:

Remember the appeal of the numerous neighbourhood pubs and tapas restaurants in Palma.

These locations provide a more laid-back atmosphere for partaking in a variety of beverages, from local wines to craft cocktails.

Marc Fosh Restaurant

Bar Bosch Cafe

Bon Lloc Veggie Restaurant

La Lonja

ensaimada

sobrassada

Tumbet

pa amb oli

CHAPTER 7

Shopping in Palma de Mallorca

Shopping Tips:

At certain periods of the year, you can discover fantastic bargains, so keep an eye out for the **"rebajas" (sales).**

The majority of stores in Palma adhere to the Spanish siesta custom, so time your shopping trips around the midday break.

Always double-check store hours because they may change, particularly on holidays and Sundays.

I.   Paseo del Borne:

High-end retailers and premium goods can be found along this lovely promenade.

Discover designer shops like Louis Vuitton, Hermès, and Carolina Herrera by taking a stroll along Paseo del Borne.

II.   Jaume III:

Jaume III is a different upmarket retail area with well-known designer labels, jewellery shops, and good dining alternatives. It's a great place to people watch and buy in luxury.

III.   Avinguda de Jaume III:

This street runs parallel to Jaume III and features a variety of high-end and mid-range retailers, including clothes, accessory, and cosmetics businesses. It's a favourite hangout for people who love fashion.

IV.   Carrer de Sant Nicolau:

This street, which is in the historic district, is lined with artisan stores and boutiques offering one-of-a-kind jewellery, pottery, and hand-made leather goods.

V.   Mercat de l'Olivar:

Foodies will like this lively food market. Fresh fruit, regional cheeses, wines, and gourmet foods are available. It's ideal for trying out regional cuisine and buying ingredients to take home.

VI.   Passeig des Born and Plaça Major:

On specific days, these charming squares hold outdoor markets with a range of products, including clothing, accessories, and handicrafts. a fantastic location for finding deals.

VII.   Santa Catalina Market:

This market, which is situated in the hip Santa Catalina neighbourhood, is well-known for its artisanal food vendors and fresh produce.

For those looking for regional ingredients and culinary delights, it is a must-stop.

VIII.   Olivar Market:

A variety of fresh produce, meats, seafood, and gourmet goods are available at this indoor market. Both locals and tourists like visiting it.

IX.   Boutiques in La Lonja:

Charming shops selling anything from clothing and accessories to one-of-a-kind home decor can be found all across the La Lonja neighbourhood. It's ideal for seeking out hidden gems.

X.   Shopping Centres:

Palma is home to a number of shopping centres, including Porto Pi Centro and Fan Mallorca Shopping, which provide a variety of international brands, clothing, gadgets, and entertainment choices.

XI.   Local Souvenirs:

- Don't forget to pick up some regional delicacies as keepsakes, such ensaimadas (pastry), Mallorcan wine, and artisanal goods made from olive and almond wood.

Local Markets

I.   Mercat de l'Olivar:

One of the most famous and active marketplaces on the island is Mercat de l'Olivar, which is situated in the centre of Palma. A food lover's heaven, this indoor market offers a huge selection of fresh fruit, fish, meats, cheeses, and baked items.

Additionally, you can discover stalls selling apparel, spices, and flowers. Both locals and tourists should visit the market because of its lively environment, which is characterised by energetic chatter and enticing scents.

II.   Santa Catalina Market:

This market, which is a favourite among locals and foodies alike, is located in the hip Santa Catalina neighbourhood. Fresh seafood, organic fruits and vegetables, as well as a selection of foreign and Spanish delicacies, are just a few of the gourmet goods sold at Santa Catalina Market.

The market's outdoor patios and tapas bars are ideal for sipping local wine while having a leisurely meal.

III.   Mercadillo de Sineu:

Visit the Mercadillo de Sineu, Mallorca's oldest and most authentic weekly market, for a taste of Mallorcan tradition and rural culture. It offers a variety of goods, including handmade items, apparel, regional delicacies, and livestock every Wednesday.

It's a great location to get a taste of the island's agricultural past and interact with the welcoming residents.

IV.   Es Mercat de Sant Juan:

In the northern section of Palma, this market showcases the finest Mediterranean cuisine. It's a terrific place to buy premium ingredients because it has a focus on organic and locally sourced goods. Fresh veggies, olive oils, specialty cheeses, and other foods are available.

Additionally, Es Mercat de Sant Juan has food stands where you can indulge in delectable dishes made with ingredients that are fresh from the market.

V.   Artisan and Flea Markets:

On particular days of the week or during special events, Palma de Mallorca hosts a large number of artisan and flea markets. These markets provide a large selection of one-of-a-kind antiques, apparel, jewellery, and crafts.

Some of the well-known ones are the Artà Market, which is well-known for its ceramics and pottery, and the Flea Market at Plaça Major.

VI.   Night Markets:

A number of night markets, including the Rata Market and the Night Market of Palma, are held in Palma throughout the summer. These markets are ideal for strolling in the evenings, buying homemade goods, and taking in live entertainment and street cuisine.

Boutique Shopping

I. **Passeig del Born:**

Passeig del Born, one of Palma's most well-known shopping alleys, is home to a number of posh retailers. High-end fashion labels, including Spanish and foreign designers, can be found here. Your shopping expedition will take place against the scenic backdrop of the tree-lined promenade, where you'll find everything from chic apparel boutiques to pricey jewellery stores.

II. **Jaime III:**

Jaime III is a bustling street dotted with businesses that provide a mix of designer and boutique brands. It is another well-liked shopping location.

It's the ideal location for shopping for apparel, accessories, and shoes. Many of the boutiques in this area concentrate on high-end, distinctive items that appeal to both traditional and modern tastes.

III.   Carrer de Sant Nicolau:

This street is a must-visit for anyone looking for independent businesses that showcase the creations of regional artisans and up-and-coming designers.

This pleasant strip is lined with boutiques selling artisan apparel, jewellery, and household goods. Unique goods can be found that are great as gifts or mementos.

IV.   Plaza Mayor Boutiques:

Plaza Mayor, a historic area surrounded by stores, cafes, and restaurants, is situated in the centre of the old town. This region is home to many boutiques that specialise in one-of-a-kind and artisanal goods such handmade leather goods, classic Spanish ceramics, and specially made apparel. The setting here enhances the charm of your shopping adventure.

V.   Soho District:

Palma's Soho neighbourhood, close to Santa Catalina, is renowned for its bohemian and artistic vibe. A variety of eccentric businesses that sell vintage apparel, original art, and accessories are located here.

For those looking for unusual and unconventional styles, it is the perfect location.

VI. Concept Stores:

There are a number of concept stores in Palma de Mallorca that include carefully curated collections of apparel, home goods, and lifestyle goods. These shops are excellent places to find cutting-edge trends because they frequently carry a mix of regional and international designers.

VII. Jewellery Boutiques:

Palma has a booming jewellery industry with boutique stores that focus on handcrafted items, if you're a jewellery connoisseur. These shops provide services for making custom jewellery as well as a variety of precious and semi-precious stones set in distinctive designs.

Souvenirs and Gifts

I. Mallorcan Rattan Products:

Weaving rattan is one of Mallorca's distinctive trades. Rattan goods come in a number of forms, including hats, backpacks, and baskets. These things normally cost between €15 and €50, depending on size and degree of design complexity.

II. Mallorcan Pearls:

Mallorca is well-known for its man-made pearls, also referred to as "Mallorcan pearls." These are made to look like real pearls and are available in a range of hues and sizes.

Simple pearl jewellery can range in price from €20 to €50, while more complex items can cost up to €100.

III. Pottery and ceramics:

The island is known for its elaborate designs and vivid colours in pottery and ceramics. Depending on the size and intricacy of the item, prices might range from €10 to €30 for tiny ornamental items to €50 to €200 or more for larger and more elaborate items.

IV. Espadrilles:

The "alpargatas," or traditional Spanish espadrilles, are a preferred option for footwear gifts. Basic versions typically cost between €10 and €20, although designer or specially manufactured espadrilles can cost €50 or more.

V. Local Food and Wine:

Mallorca produces top-notch wines, extra virgin olive oils, and gourmet foods. Local wine bottles typically cost around €10, but more expensive bottles can cost up to €30. Prices for gourmet foods and olive oils might range greatly, but you can buy high-quality items for as little as €5.

VI. Handmade Jewelry:

Mallorca provides a variety of handcrafted jewellery, including items produced with regional metals and jewels. Handmade jewellery can cost as little as €20 for simple patterns or as much as €100 for elaborate and personalised pieces.

VII. Saffron and spices:

Saffron and spices from Spain are highly regarded. Particularly saffron may be extremely pricey, with little sachets beginning at about €10. Prices for other spices and seasonings range from $2 to $5, making them more affordable.

VIII.   Local Art and Prints:

You can get regional paintings, prints, and photographs at a range of price points if you're interested in art. Prints and miniature artworks can be purchased for as little as €20, while original paintings can cost anything from €100 to several thousand.

CHAPTER 8

Outdoor Activities:

Water Sports:

I. Sailing:

The sailing conditions in Palma are world-class. The bay is ideal for both novice and expert sailors due to its mild breezes and tranquil waters. To explore the coastline and adjacent bays, you can lease a sailboat or enrol in a sailing lesson. Prestigious sailing competitions like the Copa del Rey Regatta are also held in the city.

II. Windsurfing and Kitesurfing:

Palma Bay is the perfect location for windsurfing and kitesurfing because of the predictable wind patterns there. There are places designated for these sports, as well as rentals and instruction that are easily accessible. For wind and kite surfing, the beaches of Can Pastilla and Arenal are particularly well-liked.

III. Stand-Up Paddleboarding (SUP):

Paddleboarding is a great way to discover Mallorca's tranquil, blue waters. SUP rentals and instruction are available at many beaches and water sports facilities. You may paddle along the coast, looking for undiscovered bays, and taking in the beautiful scenery.

IV. Kayaking:

A tranquil way to explore Mallorca's coastline and caves is by kayak. Sea caverns like the Cova de Coloms and the Cova des Pont can be explored using kayaks that can be rented. For those who want to discover the island's natural splendour, guided kayak tours are also offered.

V. Scuba Diving and Snorkeling:

There is an abundance of marine life and underwater scenery in the waters near Palma de Mallorca. Divers and snorkelers can explore colourful coral reefs, submerged caverns, and shipwrecks. Dive shops provide both beginner-level instruction and guided dives for certified divers.

VI. Jet Skiing and Parasailing:

You may hire a jet ski and ride the waves down the coast for an adrenaline experience. Another exhilarating choice is parasailing, which lets you soar above the water while taking in breath-blowing vistas of the coastline.

VII.   **Fishing:**

For individuals who prefer angling, fishing charters are offered. You can go fishing in the Mediterranean Sea for a variety of fish, such as tuna, dorado, and other species. Many fishing excursions offer all the required gear and knowledge.

VIII.   **Boat Tours and Catamaran Cruises:**

Consider a boat tour or catamaran cruise if you want a more leisurely time on the sea. These tours frequently involve pit stops so you can swim, snorkel, and enjoy food or drinks on board while admiring the beautiful scenery.

Hiking and Nature Trails

I.   **Serra de Tramuntana:**

The mountain range of the Serra de Tramuntana is a UNESCO World Heritage site and a hiking lover's haven. It offers a variety of trails, from strenuous treks at high altitudes to slower strolls.

The GR-221 long-distance track, which crosses the entire range, and the renowned ascent of Puig Major, the island's highest mountain, are two well-known routes.

II.   Torrent de Pareis:

This well-known walk leads you through a breathtaking limestone canyon with lofty cliffs and glistening rivers. The trail enters the gorge from the lovely village of Escorca where it begins.

Along the journey, there will be some boulder climbing and river crossings, so be prepared. It's a difficult yet extremely gratifying experience.

III.   Cap de Formentor:

Situated on the island's northernmost point, Cap de Formentor offers a beautiful coastline walk with stunning views of the Mediterranean. The route eventually arrives at a lighthouse at the cape's southernmost point after winding through pine forests and rugged rocks. Both the route and the destination are breathtaking.

IV.   Cala Boquer:

The excellent walk for families and nature lovers is this one, which is quite simple. It begins in the Port de Pollença community and takes you to the secluded Cala Boquer beach. You'll pass through beautiful terrain and take in views of the sea and the mountains in the distance as you travel.

V. Garrafó de sa Mola:

This nature reserve, which can be found in the east of Mallorca, has a network of clearly marked trails that meander through pine forests, limestone formations, and valleys.

There are paths for different skill levels, with a range in length and difficulty. The area's wide variety of avian species will be appreciated by birdwatchers as well.

V.   Albufera Nature Reserve:

Birdwatchers and other environment lovers will find this wetland reserve to be a refuge. You may explore the varied ecosystems, including marshes, reed beds, and lagoons, via a number of pathways and boardwalks. It's a great location for seeing wildlife and waterfowl.

VI. Talaia d'Albercutx:

Hike to the Talaia d'Albercutx, a hill overlooking the Bay of Pollença, with panoramic views of the sea and rocky coastline. The trail is well-known for its breathtaking sunset views and offers a mixture of rough terrain and lush foliage.

Golfing

I. Golf Courses:

Palma de Mallorca and its surrounding areas are home to several exceptional golf courses. A few of the most notable ones include:

II. Golf Son Vida:

Located just outside Palma, this historic course is one of the oldest in Mallorca. It features lush fairways, challenging greens, and stunning views of the surrounding mountains.

III. Golf Son Muntaner:

Part of the Arabella Golf Mallorca complex, this course offers a challenging layout with water hazards and beautiful landscaping. It's known for its impeccable course conditions.

IV. Golf Park Mallorca Puntiró:

This championship course is situated inland, offering a tranquil golfing experience. It's known for its wide fairways and natural surroundings.

V. Golf Santa Ponsa:

With three different courses to choose from, including the Santa Ponsa I, II, and III, this golf club provides a variety of playing experiences. The courses feature picturesque views of the sea and mountains.

VI. Golf Alcanada:

Located in the north of the island, Golf Alcanada boasts incredible views of the Bay of Alcúdia and the lighthouse on Alcanada Island. It's known for its pristine course conditions and challenging design.

- **Weather:**

Mallorca's Mediterranean climate makes it an ideal year-round golfing destination. Summers are warm and sunny, while winters are mild, allowing golfers to enjoy the sport virtually any time of the year. However, spring and autumn are particularly pleasant for golfing due to milder temperatures.

- **Golf Services:**

Most golf courses in Palma de Mallorca offer comprehensive facilities, including clubhouses, driving ranges, putting greens, and rental equipment. Many also provide golf academies and professional instructors for golfers of all skill levels.

- Tournaments and Events:

Mallorca hosts various golf tournaments and events throughout the year, attracting both amateur and professional golfers. These events provide an opportunity to witness top-level golf and perhaps even participate in local competitions.

- Dining and Relaxation:

After a round of golf, you can unwind at the golf course's clubhouse or restaurant, where you can savor local cuisine and enjoy scenic views. Many clubs offer spa and wellness facilities for a relaxing post-game experience.

- Booking and Tee Times:

It's advisable to book tee times in advance, especially during the high season (spring and autumn). Most golf courses have online booking systems or you can contact them directly to secure your spot.

- **Transportation:**

Palma de Mallorca has a well-connected airport, making it easy to access the golf courses on the island. Additionally, many golf clubs offer shuttle services from popular tourist areas.

Cycling

I.   Bike Routes and Trails:

Palma de Mallorca and its surroundings offer a wide range of cycling routes to suit all preferences:

II.   Coastal Routes:

Enjoy scenic rides along the coast, taking in breathtaking sea views and the refreshing Mediterranean breeze. Popular coastal routes include the journey from Palma to Playa de

Palma, as well as the coastal roads to Cala Millor and Alcúdia.

III.   Mountain Trails:

For more adventurous riders, the Tramuntana mountain range offers challenging climbs and thrilling descents. The famous Sa Calobra climb and the ascent to the Puig Major are favorites among experienced cyclists.

IV.   Inland Villages:

Explore Mallorca's charming inland villages by bike. Routes that take you through quaint villages like Sineu, Petra, and Algaida allow you to experience the island's culture and heritage.

V.   Bike Rentals and Services:

Palma de Mallorca has numerous bike rental shops, making it easy to find the right bike for your needs. Many of these shops offer a variety of bicycles, from road bikes and mountain bikes to e-bikes and hybrids. You can also rent accessories like helmets, locks, and bike racks.

VI. Cycling Events and Tours:

Mallorca hosts various cycling events and tours throughout the year, attracting cyclists from around the world. These events range from leisurely rides to challenging races. Some popular events include the Mallorca 312 and the Mallorca 312 Kids.

VII. Safety and Etiquette:

Cyclists should always prioritize safety by wearing helmets and following traffic rules. Mallorca is generally bike-friendly, with designated cycling lanes on many roads. However, it's essential to be cautious, especially in high-traffic areas.

VIII. Cafes and Pit Stops:

Mallorca is dotted with quaint cafes and restaurants that are perfect for refueling during your ride. You'll find many cyclist-friendly establishments where you can enjoy a coffee, a hearty meal, or a taste of local cuisine.

IX. Bike-Friendly Accommodations:

Several hotels and accommodations on the island cater to cyclists, offering secure bike storage, maintenance facilities, and information on local routes. Look for hotels with the "bike-friendly" label.

X.   Weather and Timing:

The best times for cycling in Mallorca are spring (March to May) and autumn (September to November) when temperatures are pleasant, and there are fewer tourists. Summers can be hot, so early morning or late afternoon rides are advisable during this season.

XI.   Renting Guided Tours and Services:

If you're new to the island or prefer a guided experience, consider booking a guided cycling tour. Many companies offer guided rides that cater to various skill levels and interests, ensuring you make the most of your cycling adventure.

Boat Tours and Excursions

I. Coastal Cruises:

The coastline of Palma is lined with beautiful beaches, rocks, and caverns. Coastal cruises offer the ideal way to take in the natural splendour. Oftentimes, these journeys include pit breaks in quaint coastal towns where you can go swimming, sunbathe and eat the local fare.

II. Catamaran and Sailing Tours:

Sailing and catamaran cruises are well-liked for their tranquil setting and personal experience. Sunset cruises, day trips to neighbouring islands like Cabrera, or even private charters for a more individualised experience are among the possibilities available to you. These excursions frequently include possibilities for paddleboarding and snorkelling.

III.   Glass-Bottom Boat Tours:

Glass-bottom boat excursions are a great choice if you want to learn more about the underwater world without getting wet. Because of their translucent hulls, these boats let you see the vibrant marine life and underwater scenery, such as coral reefs and shipwrecks.

IV.   Dolphin and Whale Watching:

Marine life can be found in abundance around Palma de Mallorca. Tours that focus on dolphin and whale viewing offer the chance to see these wonderful animals in their natural settings. Being able to see these marine mammals playing in the surf would be an exciting experience.

V. Fishing Trips:

Those who prefer fishing can go on half-day or full-day outings where they can try their luck at catching a variety of species, such as tuna, dorado, and more. Many trips include everything you need, including culinary services for your fresh catch.

VI. Speedboat and Jet Ski Tours:

Think about taking a speedboat or jet ski excursion for an adrenaline thrill. You can travel quickly down the coast to explore hidden coves and caverns that are inaccessible to larger vessels. For those who prefer a more independent trip, jet ski rentals are also offered.

VII. Private Yacht Charters:

If you're searching for a posh and exclusive experience, you can hire a captain and crew for a private yacht. With this choice, you can create a unique itinerary for your trip and spend time with friends or family.

VIII.   Guided Tours and Excursions:

Numerous boat cruises and excursions in Palma de Mallorca include experienced guides who share details about the region's history, culture, and nature. They can improve your trip by providing you with amusing information and tales as you go.

IX.   Booking and Availability:

Scheduling boat trips and excursions in advance is a smart idea, especially during the busiest travel period. Numerous businesses provide online booking options, and you may also find out about availability via neighbourhood tour operators or your lodging.

X.   Safety Considerations:

Make sure the tour operator supplies life jackets and follows safety procedures because your safety is very important. To ensure a secure and enjoyable experience, pay heed to any directions given by the crew.

CHAPTER 9

Day Trips and Excursions

Valldemossa

This charming mountain town is well-known for its cobblestone lanes, ancient buildings, and the Royal Charterhouse of Valldemossa. Visitors can stroll through the picturesque alleyways, see the former monastery where George Sand and Frederic Chopin once lived, and eat local fare at cafes.

Sóller and the Sóller Train

A beautiful day trip from Palma is to the old village of Sóller, famous for its orange groves. From Palma to Sóller, you can travel on the historic Sóller train while taking in the beautiful scenery. Explore the town square in Sóller, go to the Sant Bartomeu Church, and eat some of the city's well-known ice creams.

I.   Cala Pi and Es Trenc Beaches:

If you're searching for unspoiled beaches, think about visiting Cala Pi and Es Trenc. Es Trenc is well-known for its long sandy shoreline and clean waters, while Cala Pi is famous for its spectacular cove with turquoise waters. Both are excellent for a leisurely beach day.

II.   Caves of Drach (Cuevas del Drach):

These caverns are a wonder of underground structures and are situated on Mallorca's eastern shore. The stalactite-filled chambers can be explored, a boat trip on the subterranean lake can be taken, and a concert of classical music can be heard inside the caverns.

III.   Artà:

This quaint village in Mallorca's northeast is rich in culture and history. Visit the Church of Transfiguració del Senyor, stroll through the mediaeval streets, and climb to the Santuari de Sant Salvador for sweeping views of the region.

IV.   Cabrera Island:

Experience untainted natural beauty by taking a boat ride to Cabrera Island, a designated national park. The island is home to a wide variety of plants and animals, such as lizards, seagulls, and aquatic life. Its waters are very clean, perfect for swimming and snorkelling, and you may go on guided trips there.

V. Wine Tasting in Binissalem:

Binissalem is a significant wine district on the island of Mallorca, which is well-known for its wine production. Take a day excursion to discover nearby wineries, sample Mallorcan wines, and discover the history of the island's winemaking.

VI. Deià:

Artists and authors have always been drawn to this quaint town on Mallorca's northwest coast. Discover the winding streets, go to the Robert Graves Museum, and enjoy the breathtaking Mediterranean vistas.

VII. Andratx and Port d'Andratx:

Explore the lovely southwest coast towns of Andratx and Port d'Andratx. Take advantage of the marina, eat at waterfront establishments, and stroll through the old town.

VIII. Cala Figuera:

This peaceful fishing community on Mallorca's southeast coast provides a window into the local way of life. Take a stroll around the charming harbour, observe the fisherman at work, and indulge in local eateries' delicious seafood.

CHAPTER 10

Conclusion

Finally, it should be noted that Palma de Mallorca is a place that genuinely captures the attention of tourists from all over the world. A unique fusion of history, culture, natural beauty, and contemporary charm can be found in this captivating Mediterranean gem, which is hidden in the Balearic archipelago. By the time we reach the last few pages of this Palma de Mallorca travel guide, it should be clear that this idyllic island is much more than just a place to relax in the sun; it is a place that has a profound impact on all who are fortunate enough to travel there.

The long history of Palma, which dates back thousands of years, is evidence of its enduring appeal. The city's past is imprinted in its cobblestone streets, historic structures, and historical defences, from the prehistoric Phoenician and Roman settlements through the Moorish influence and subsequent Christian conquests. With its breathtaking Gothic architecture, the beautiful Palma Cathedral serves as a testament to the city's tenacity and the skill of its residents throughout the ages.

However, Palma is more than just a living museum; it is a flourishing and dynamic city with an active arts scene, mouthwatering cuisine, and a friendly ambiance that embraces guests as if they were long-lost friends. The Old Town's winding streets, vibrant markets, and quaint cafes are great places to learn about the local culture, while the upscale boutiques and high-end stores along Paseo del Borne are suitable for those who enjoy luxury.

Beyond the city walls, Palma de Mallorca's natural beauty is clearly seen. There are countless options for outdoor experiences on the island because of its different landscapes, which range from pristine beaches with clear waters to rocky mountain ranges and productive vineyards. The island's natural treasures will wow you whether you're sailing down the coast, exploring the Serra de Tramuntana, or just relaxing on the sun-drenched sands.

Furthermore, Palma de Mallorca is a culinary paradise with mouthwatering fusions of foreign and Mediterranean influences. The city offers a gastronomic adventure that will please even the most discriminating palates, with everything from traditional tapas to the freshest seafood, fine dining restaurants to cosy neighbourhood tavernas.

It's crucial to stress as we draw to a close this travel guide that Palma de Mallorca is not a place for just one kind of traveller. It offers leisure to families searching for some downtime, thrill-seekers yearning for culture, and lovers looking for a romantic getaway. Palma provides a wide range of experiences that will leave you with priceless memories, whether you choose to explore historical places, indulge in regional cuisine, relax on the beach, or go hiking through breathtaking landscapes.

The only things that rival each other in Palma de Mallorca's pace of life are the gentle lapping of the Mediterranean waves and the constant warmth of the sun. Therefore, Palma de Mallorca promises an experience that goes above and beyond the usual and satisfies your intense feeling of wanderlust whether you're planning your first trip or returning for another wonderful adventure.

I wish you, just like Natalie, a voyage of exploration, amazement, and the enduring magic that makes this jewel of the Mediterranean a place unlike any other. Enjoy the splendour of the past, savour the abundance of the present, and anticipate the experiences that this entrancing island has in store for you. With its eternal charm, Palma de Mallorca will always be waiting to show you new wonders and tell you new tales.

Printed in Great Britain
by Amazon

44409047R00086